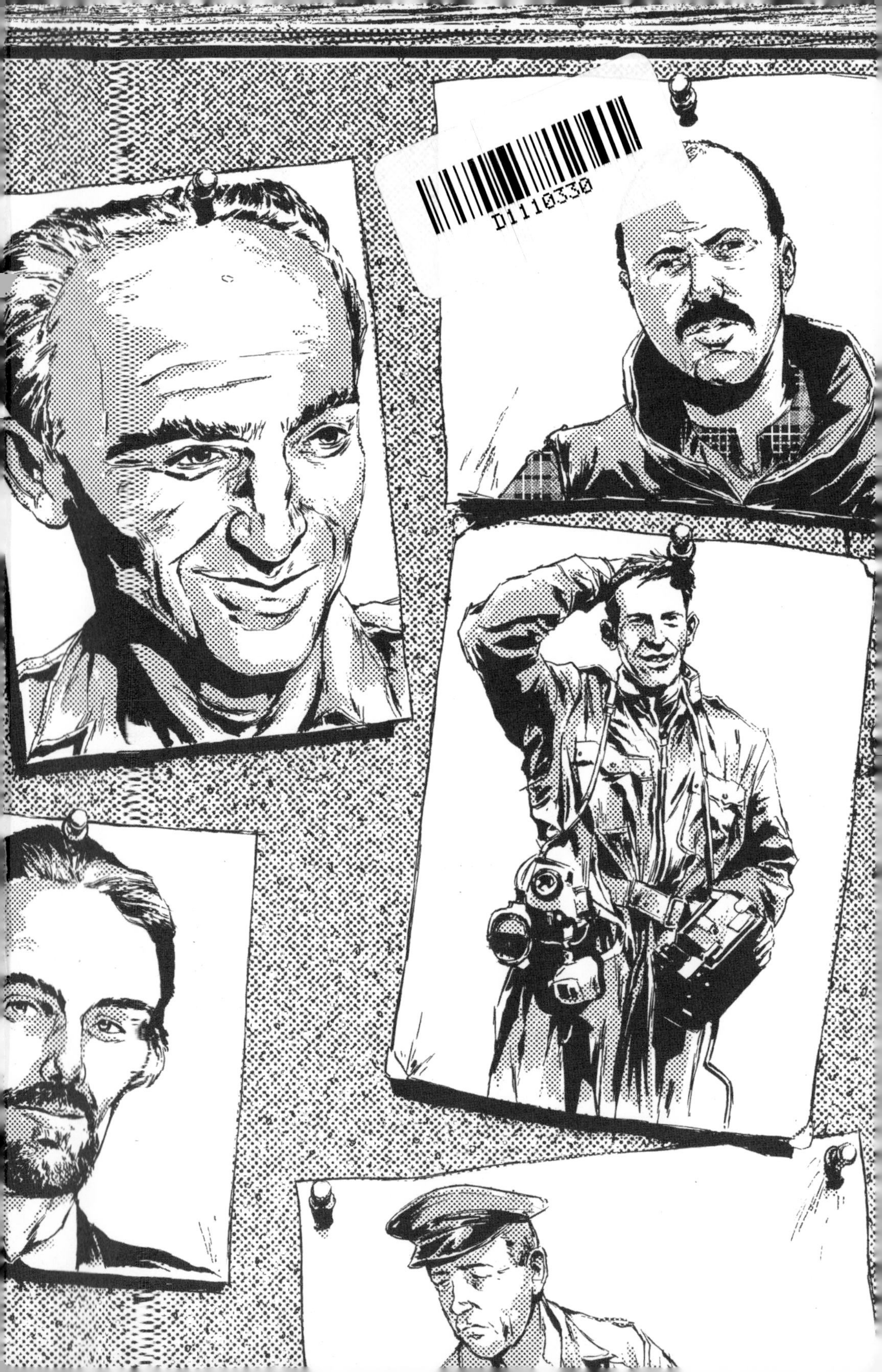

4/7

WAR-FIX

NBM Comics Lit

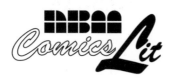

Also available in this series:
Silk Road to Ruin, $22.95
Johnny Jihad, $9.95
P&H: $3 1st item, $1 each addt'l.

We have over 200 titles,
write for our color catalog:
NBM
555 8th Ave., Suite 1202
New York, NY 10018
www.nbmpublishing.com

SILK ROAD TO RUIN
IS CENTRAL ASIA THE NEW MIDDLE EAST?
TED RALL

Johnny Jihad
RYAN INZANA
October 3rd, 1994
a graphic novel

ISBN-10: 1-56163-463-8
ISBN-13: 978-1-56163-463-7

Book design by Steven Olexa
printed in Singapore

3 2 1

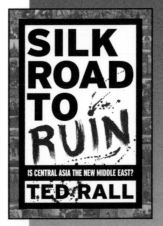

ComicsLit is an imprint
and trademark of

NANTIER • BEALL • MINOUSTCHINE
Publishing inc.
new york

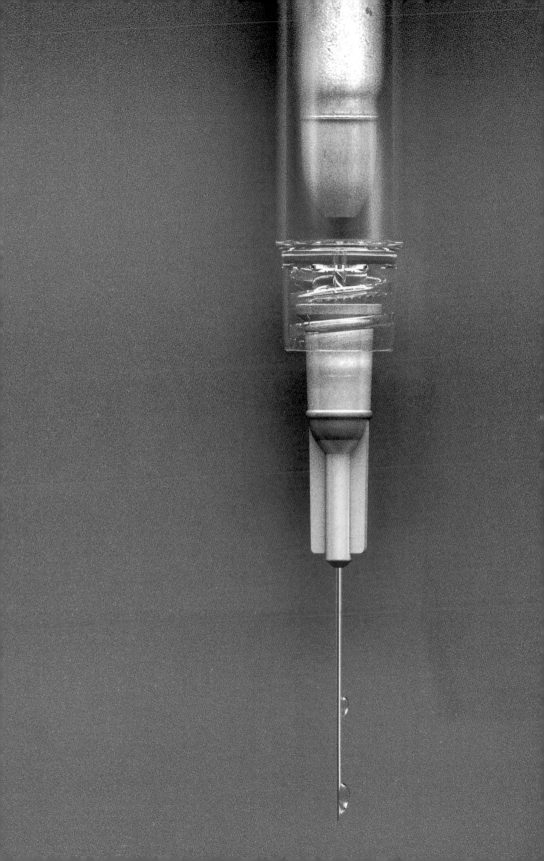

STORY / ILLUSTRATION
DAVID AXE / STEVEN OLEXA

WAR-FIX

JANUARY, 1991

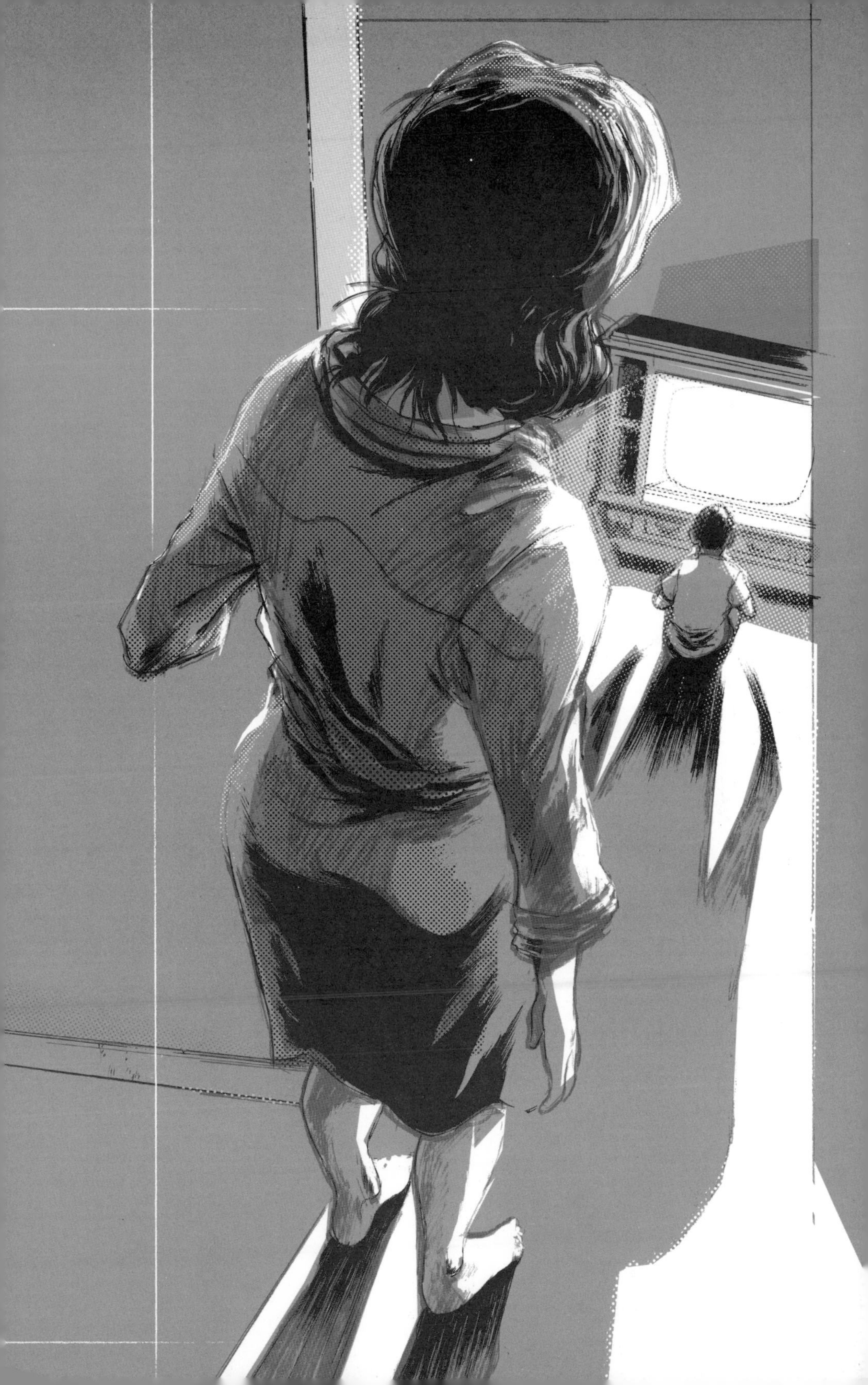

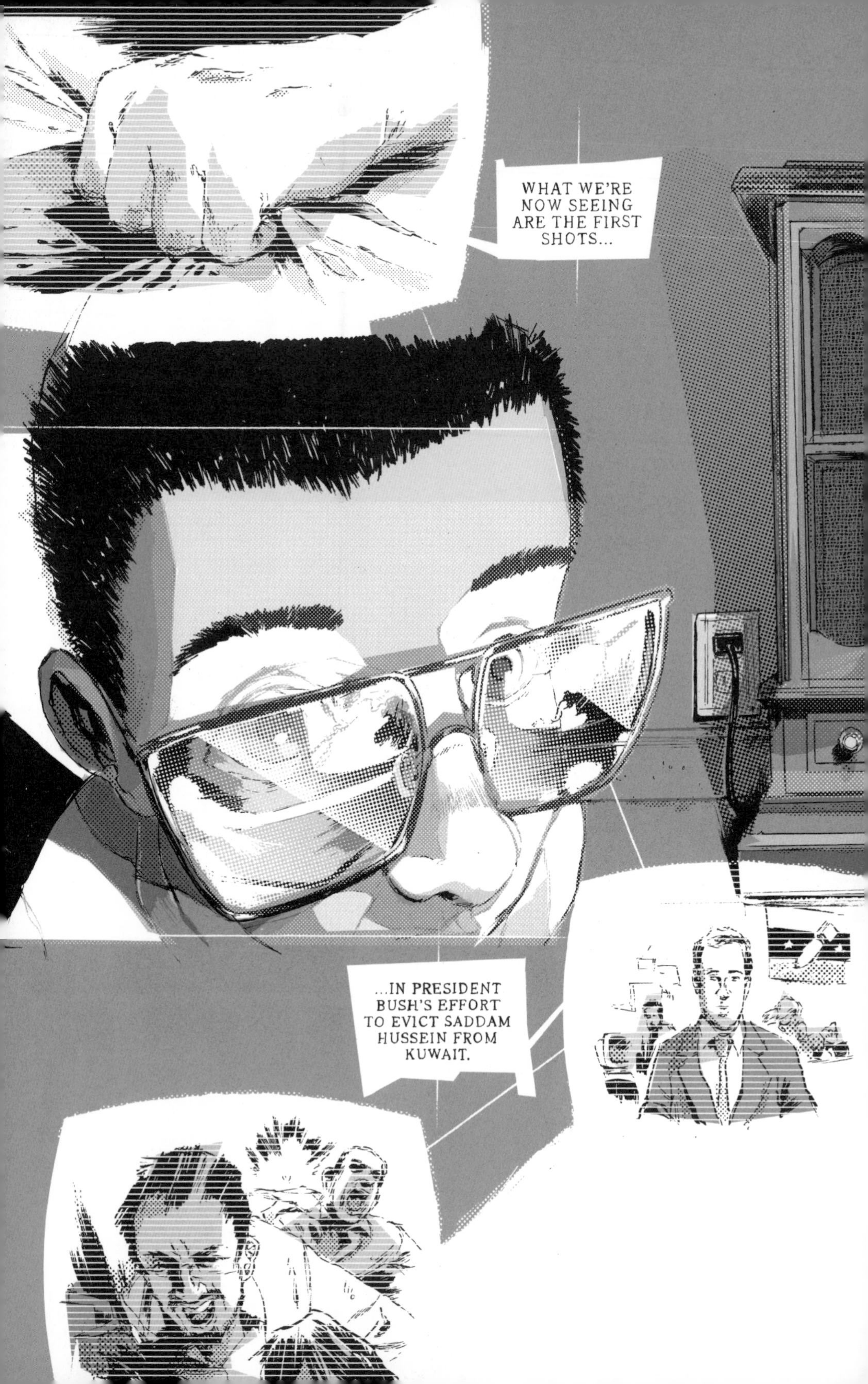
WHAT WE'RE NOW SEEING ARE THE FIRST SHOTS...
...IN PRESIDENT BUSH'S EFFORT TO EVICT SADDAM HUSSEIN FROM KUWAIT.

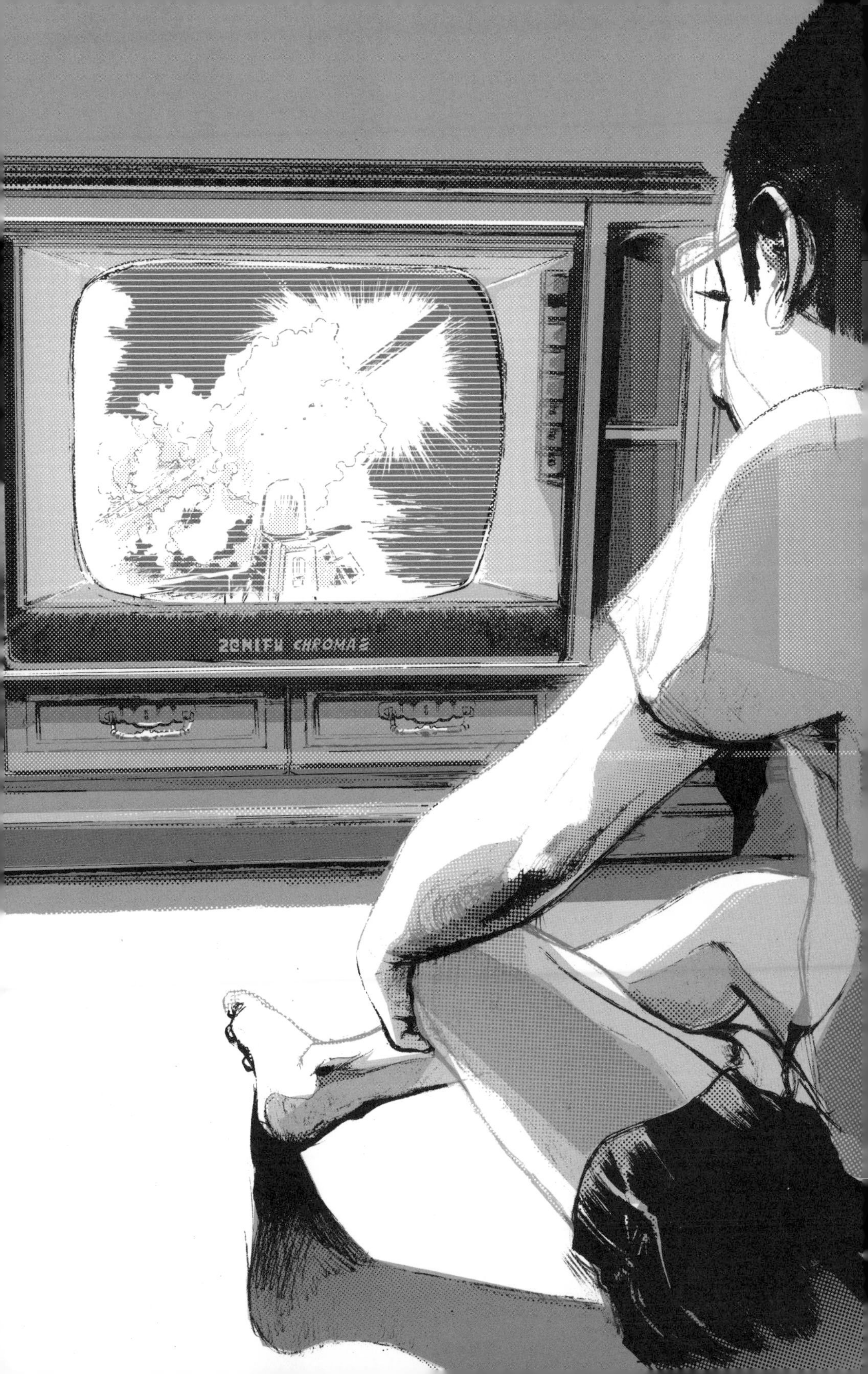

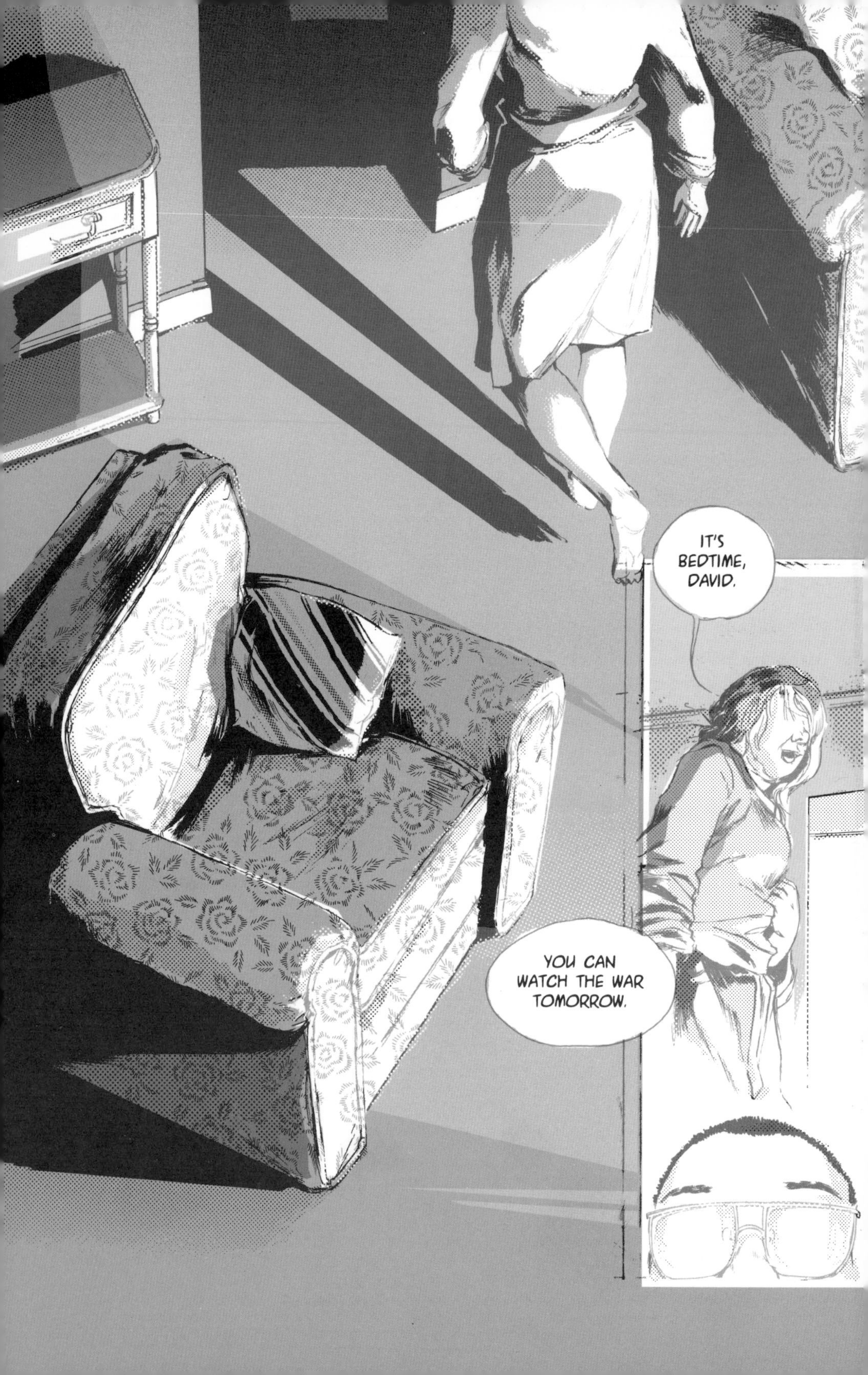
IT'S BEDTIME, DAVID.
YOU CAN WATCH THE WAR TOMORROW.

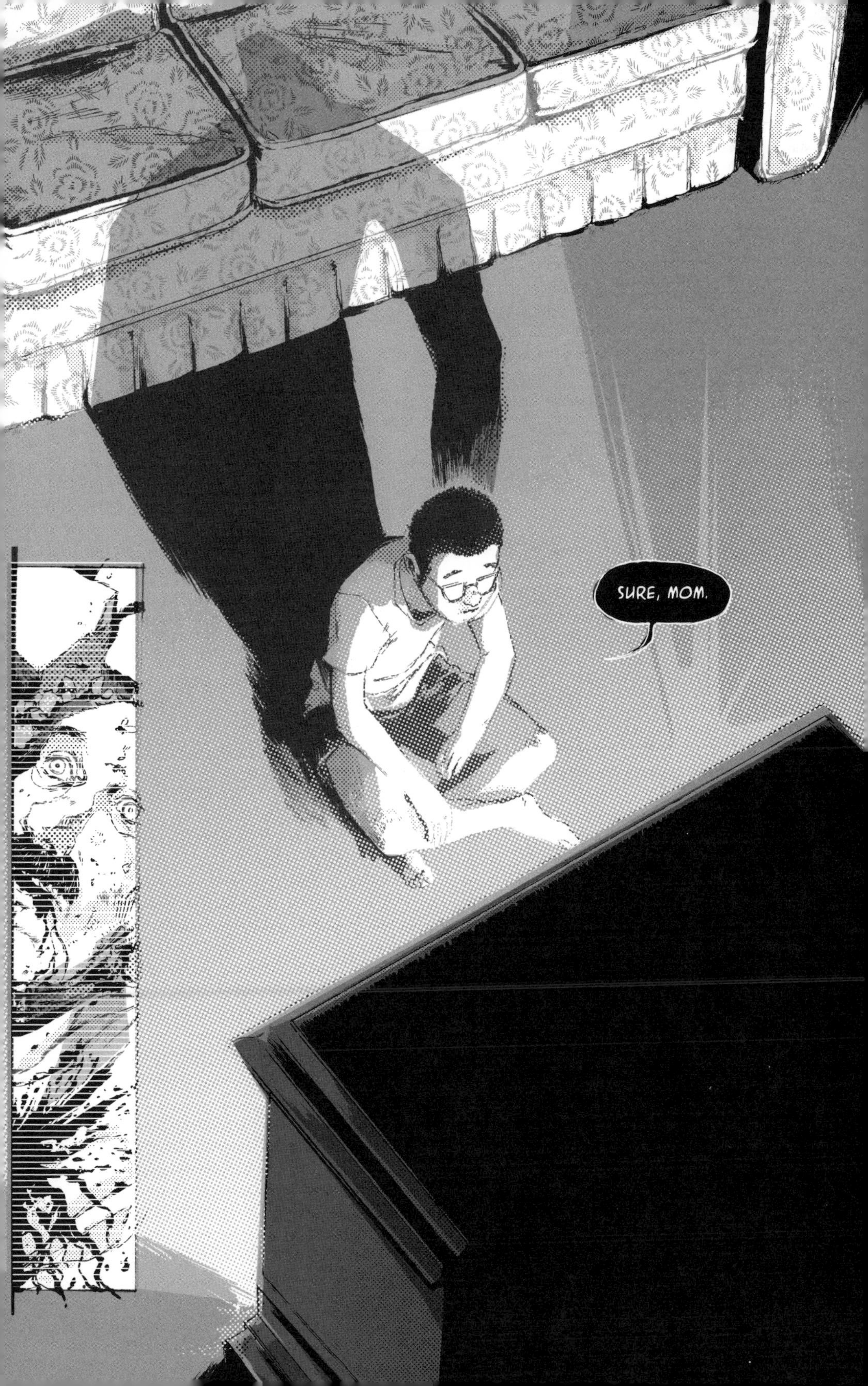
SURE, MOM.

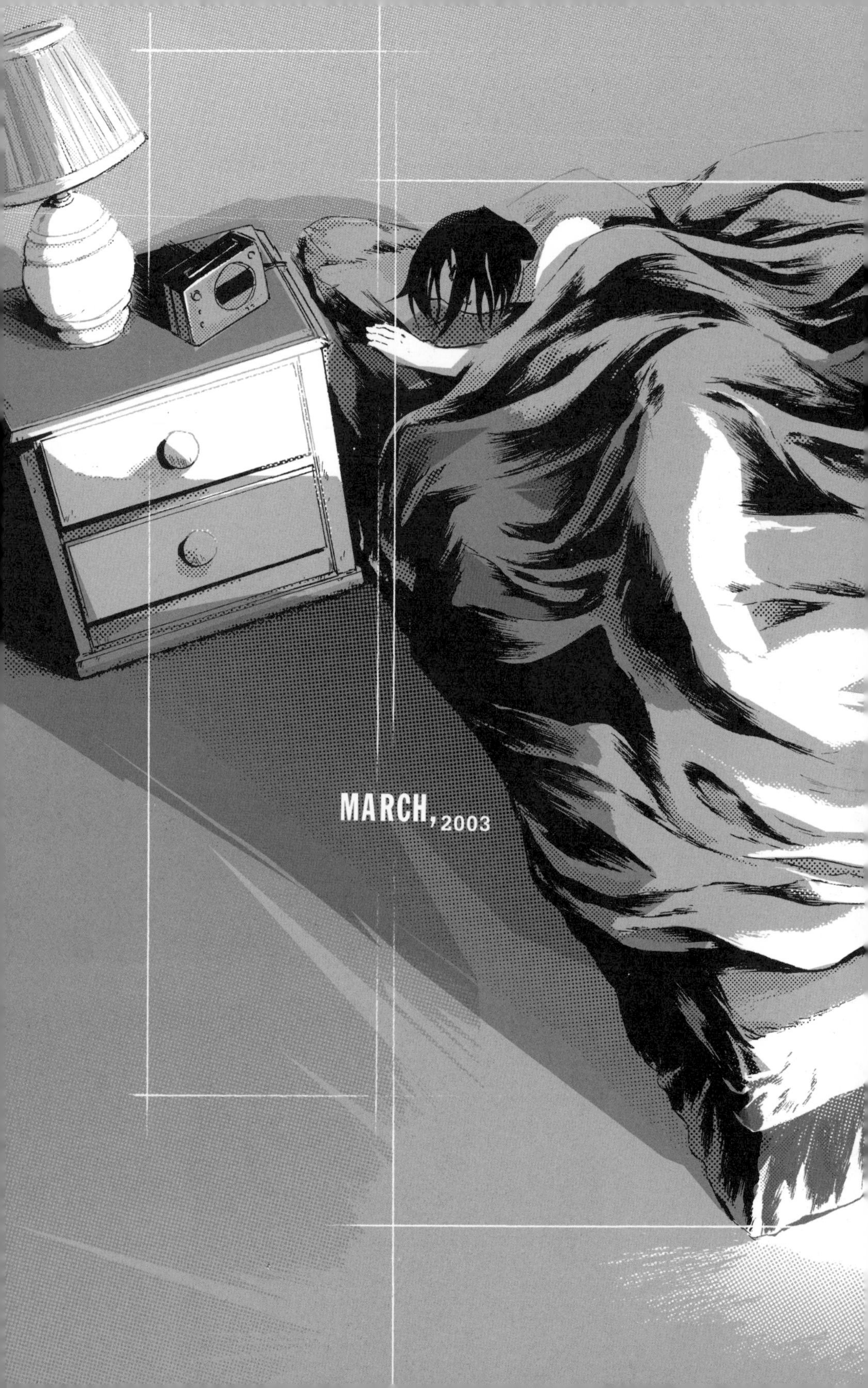
MARCH, 2003

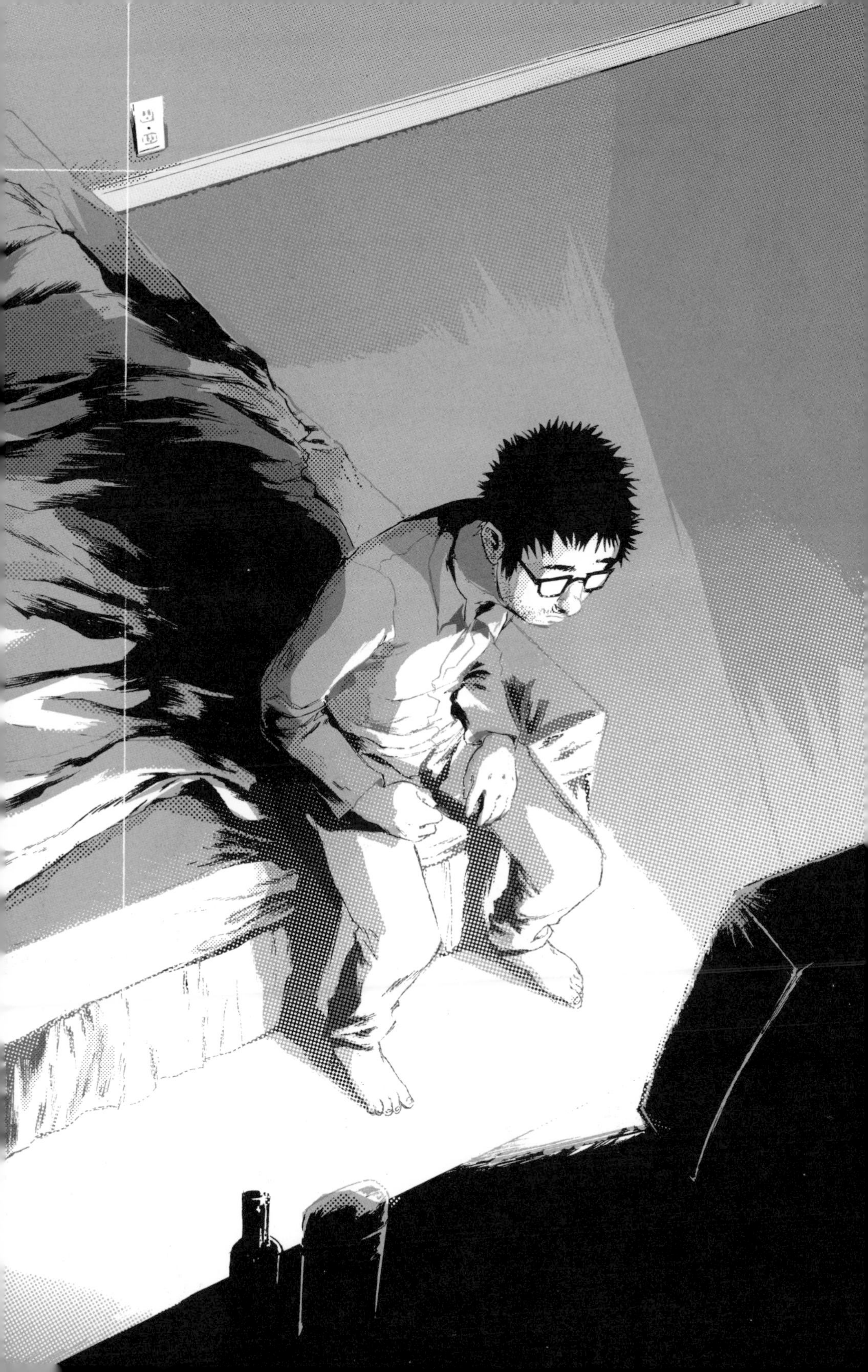

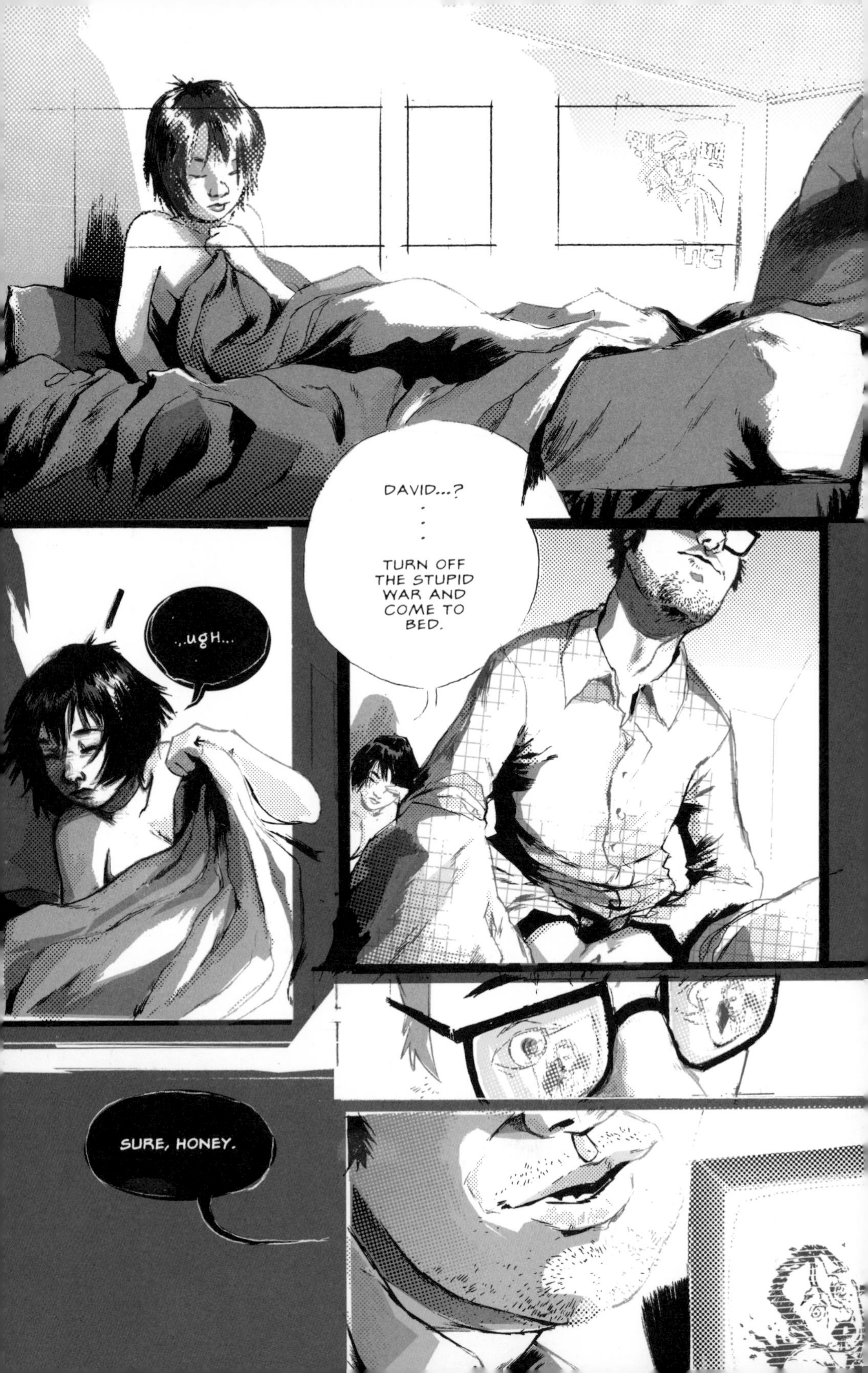
DAVID...?
.
.
.
TURN OFF THE STUPID WAR AND COME TO BED.
..UGH...
SURE, HONEY.

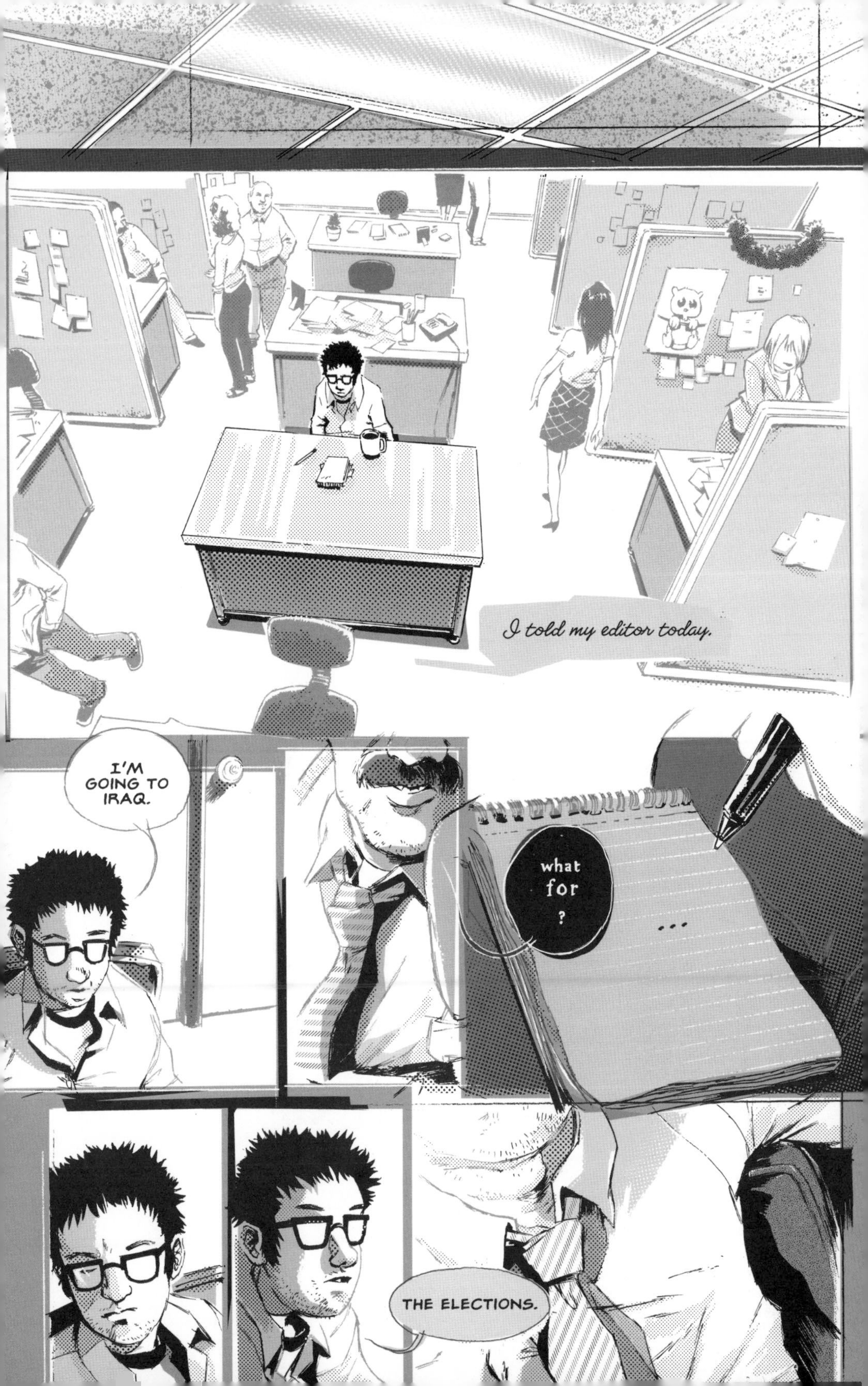
I told my editor today.
I'M GOING TO IRAQ.
what for ?
...
THE ELECTIONS.

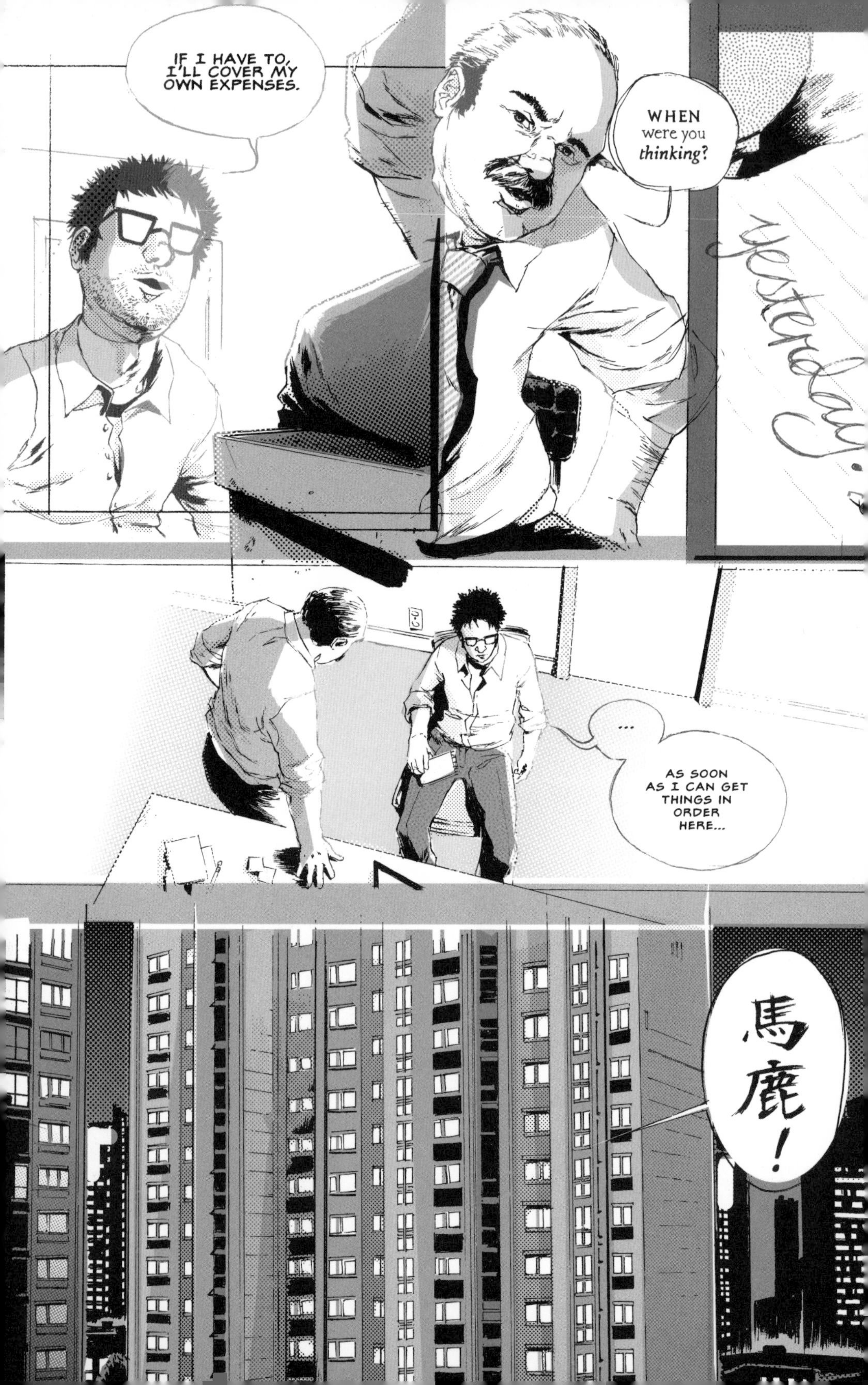
IF I HAVE TO, I'LL COVER MY OWN EXPENSES.
WHEN were you *thinking*?
yesterday?
...
AS SOON AS I CAN GET THINGS IN ORDER HERE...
馬鹿!

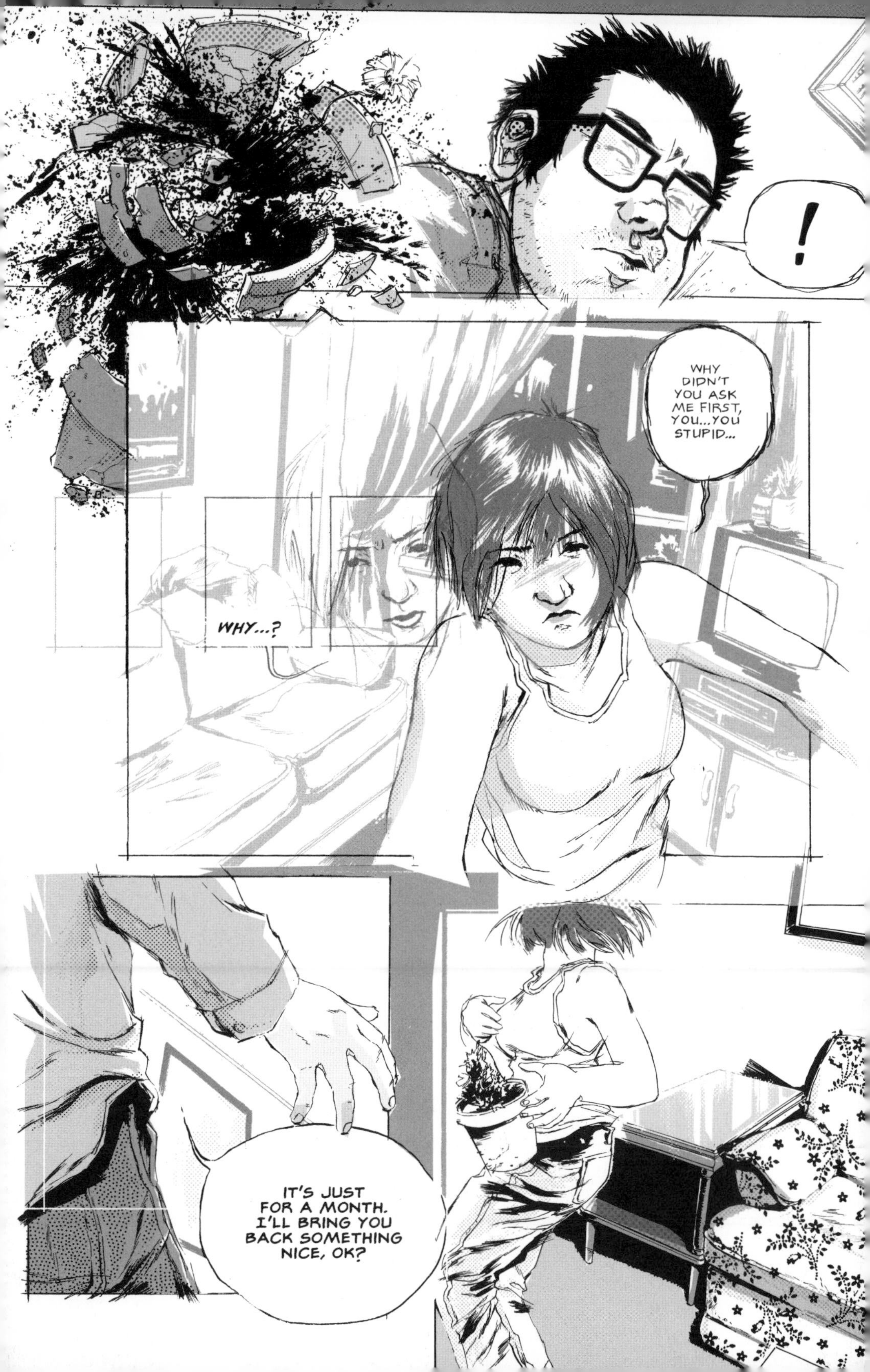
!
WHY...?
WHY DIDN'T YOU ASK ME FIRST, YOU...YOU STUPID...
IT'S JUST FOR A MONTH. I'LL BRING YOU BACK SOMETHING NICE, OK?

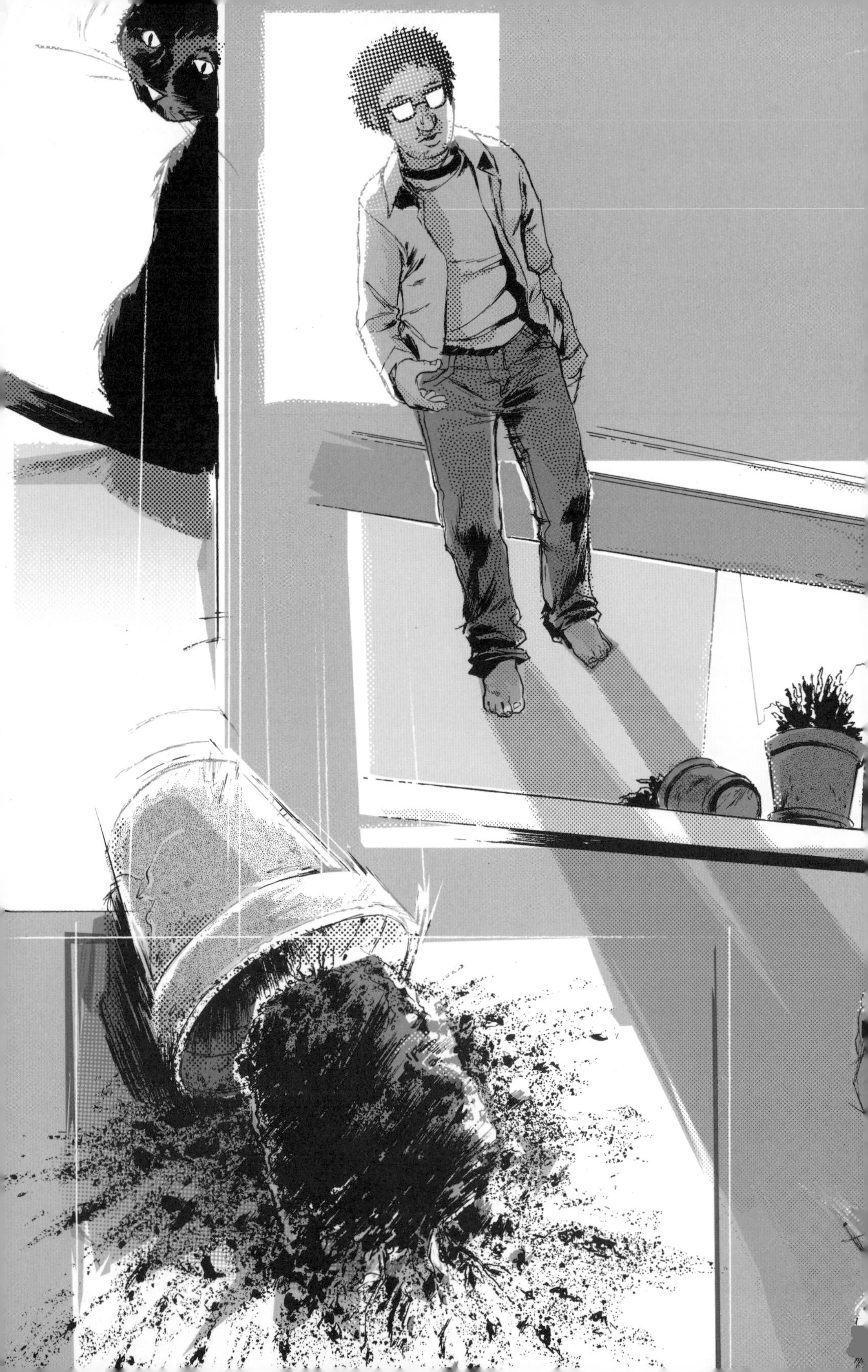

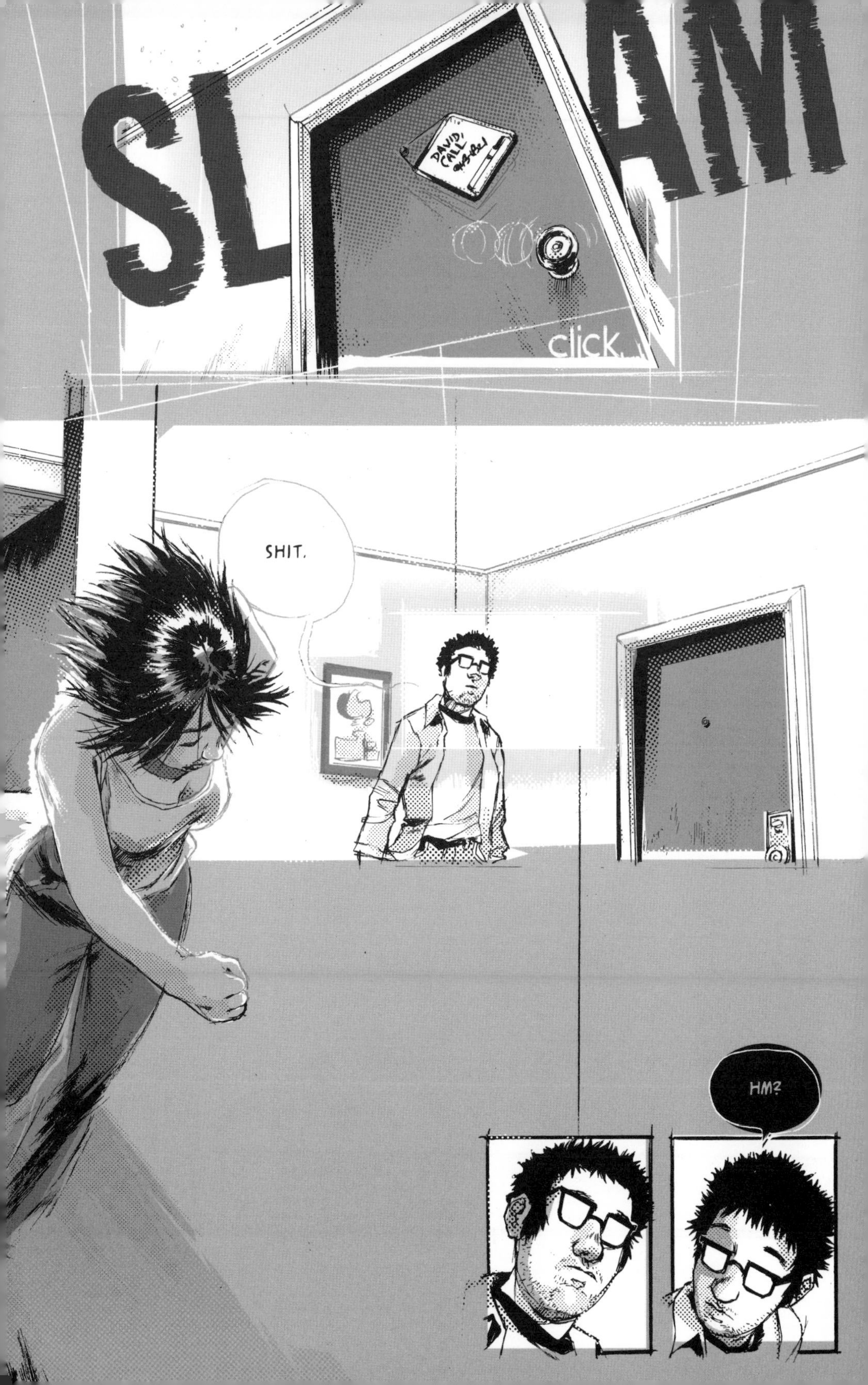
SLAM
DAVID, CALL
click.
SHIT.
HM?

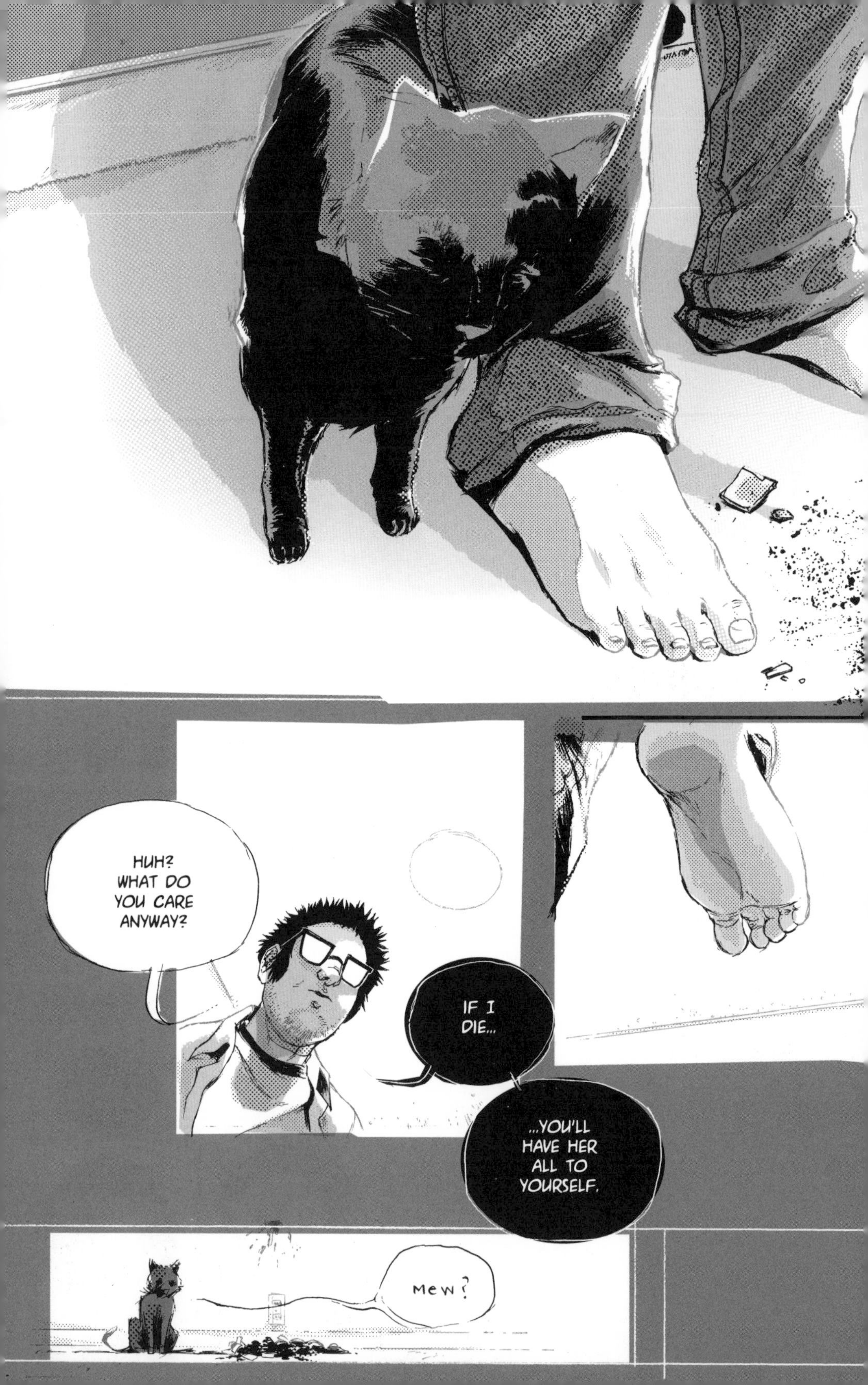
HUH? WHAT DO YOU CARE ANYWAY?
IF I DIE...
...YOU'LL HAVE HER ALL TO YOURSELF.
Mew?

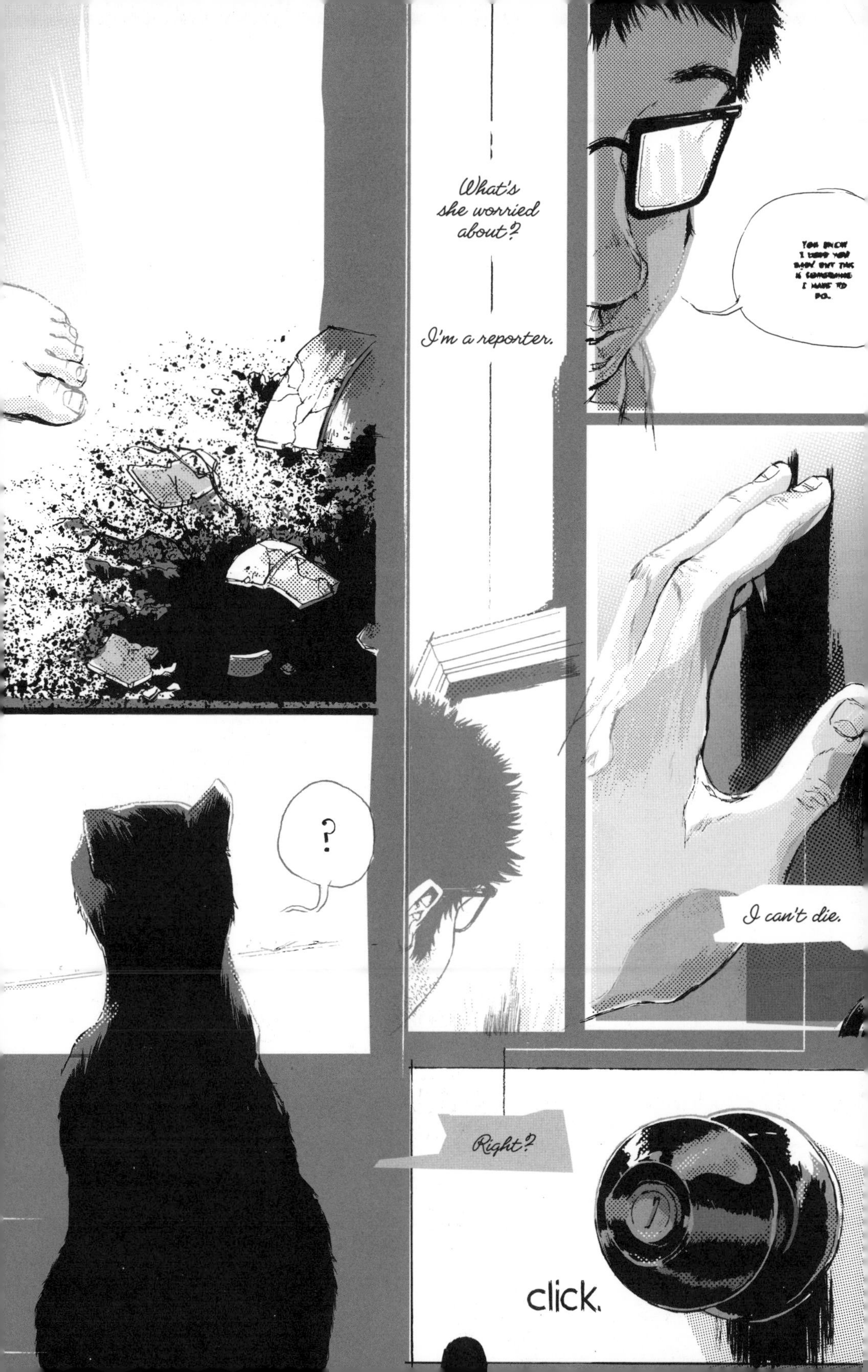
?
What's she worried about?
I'm a reporter.
I can't die.
Right?
click.

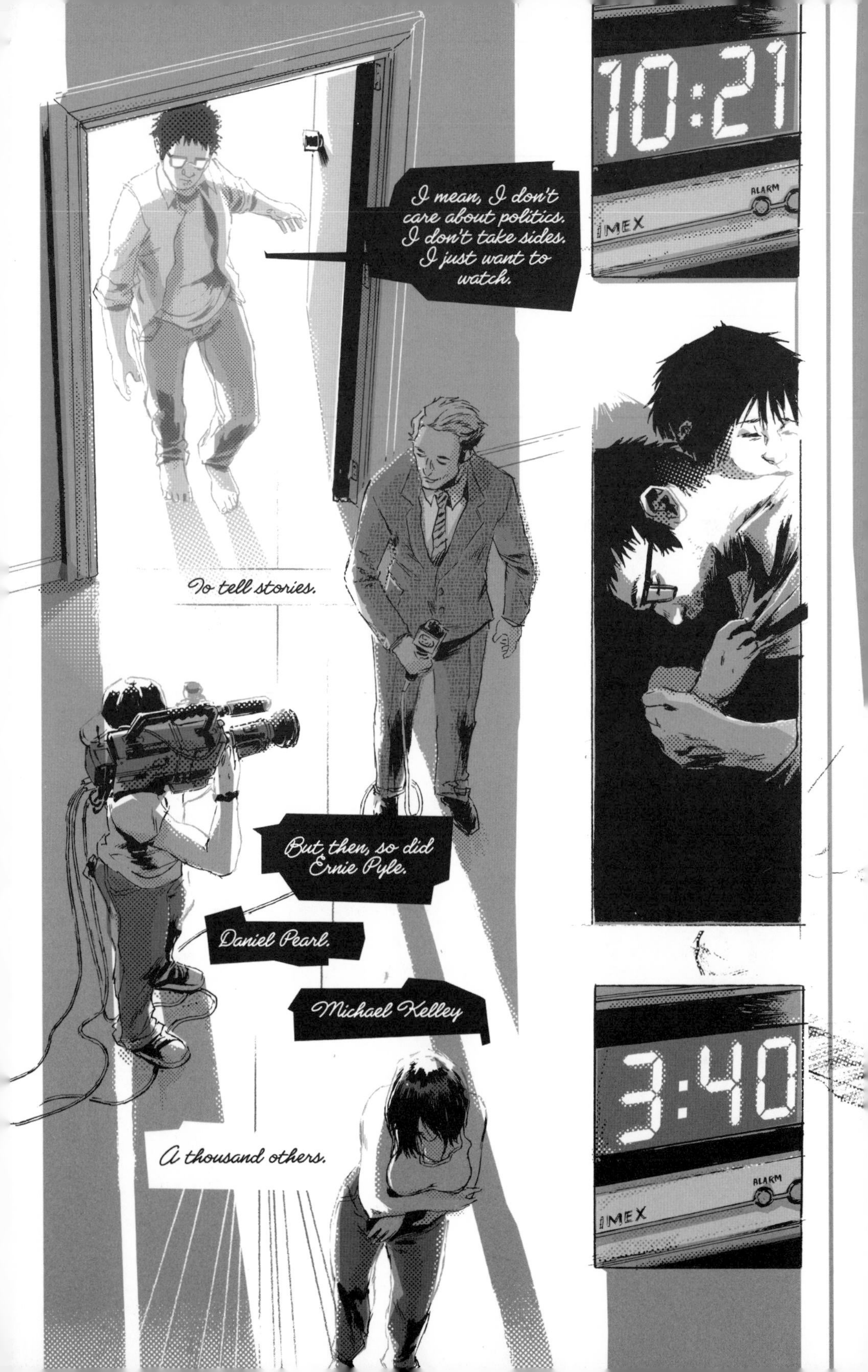

10:21
ALARM
IMEX
I mean, I don't care about politics. I don't take sides. I just want to watch.
To tell stories.
But then, so did Ernie Pyle.
Daniel Pearl.
Michael Kelley
A thousand others.
3:40
ALARM
IMEX

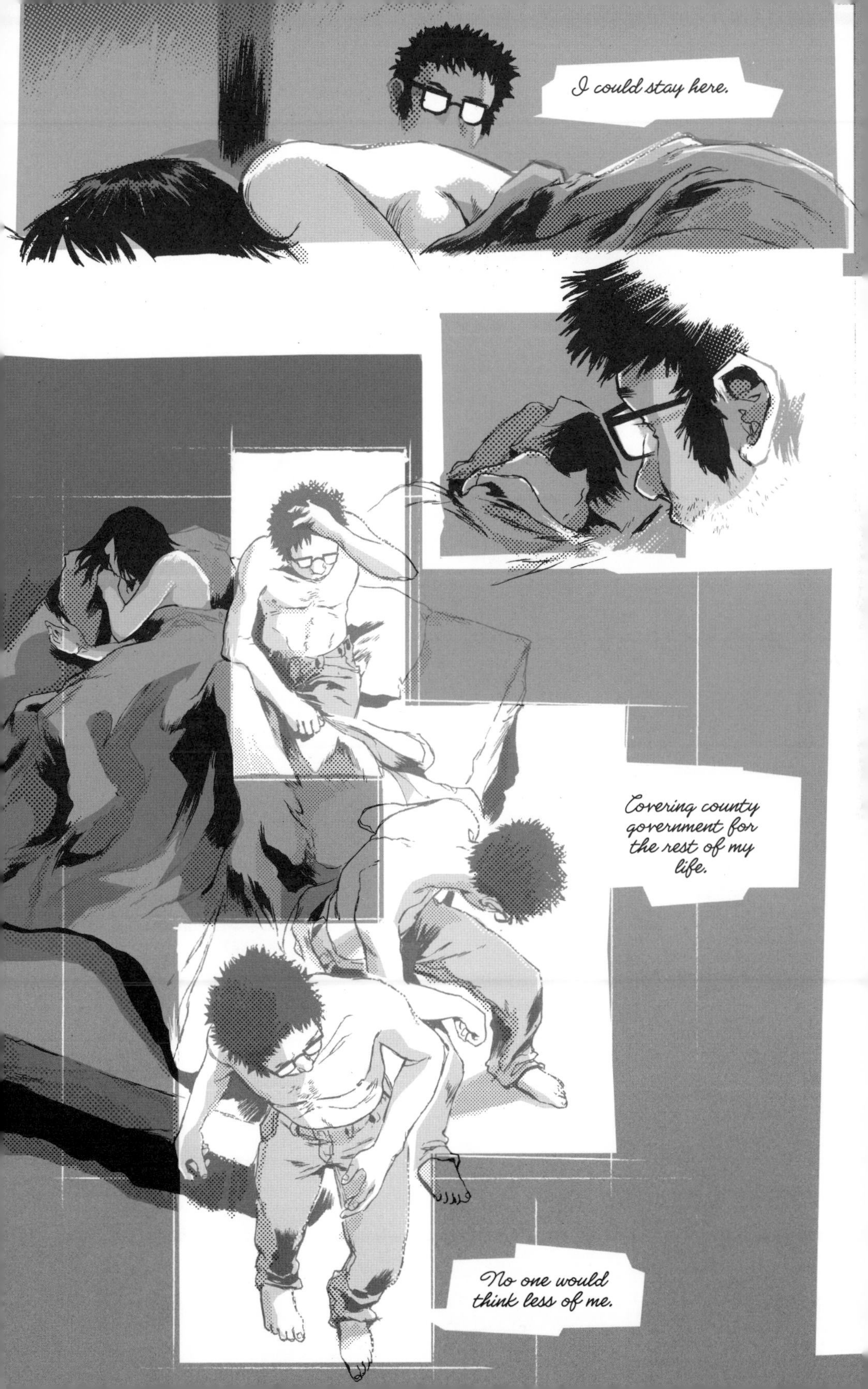
I could stay here.
Covering county government for the rest of my life.
No one would think less of me.

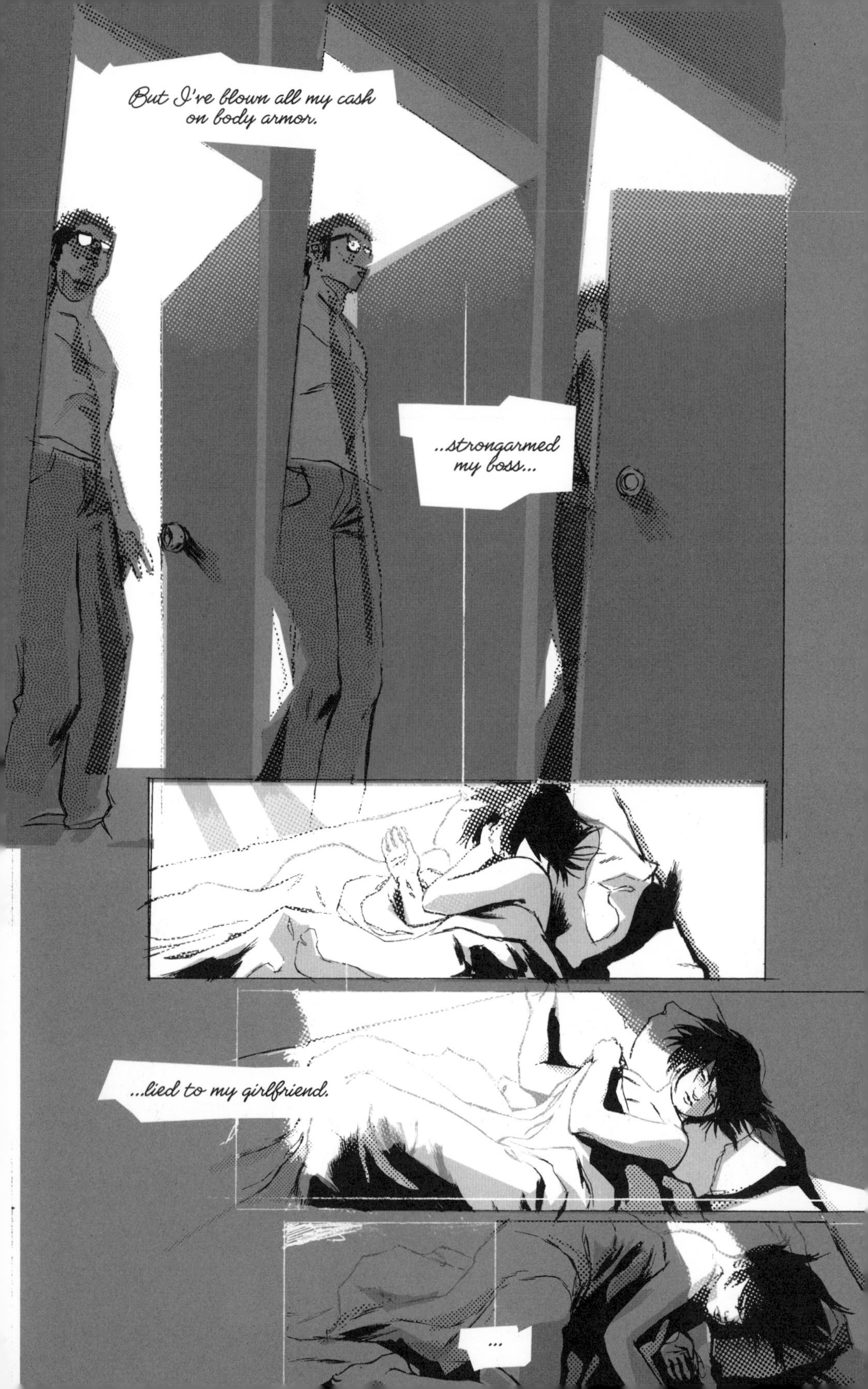
But I've blown all my cash on body armor.
..strongarmed my boss...
...lied to my girlfriend.
...

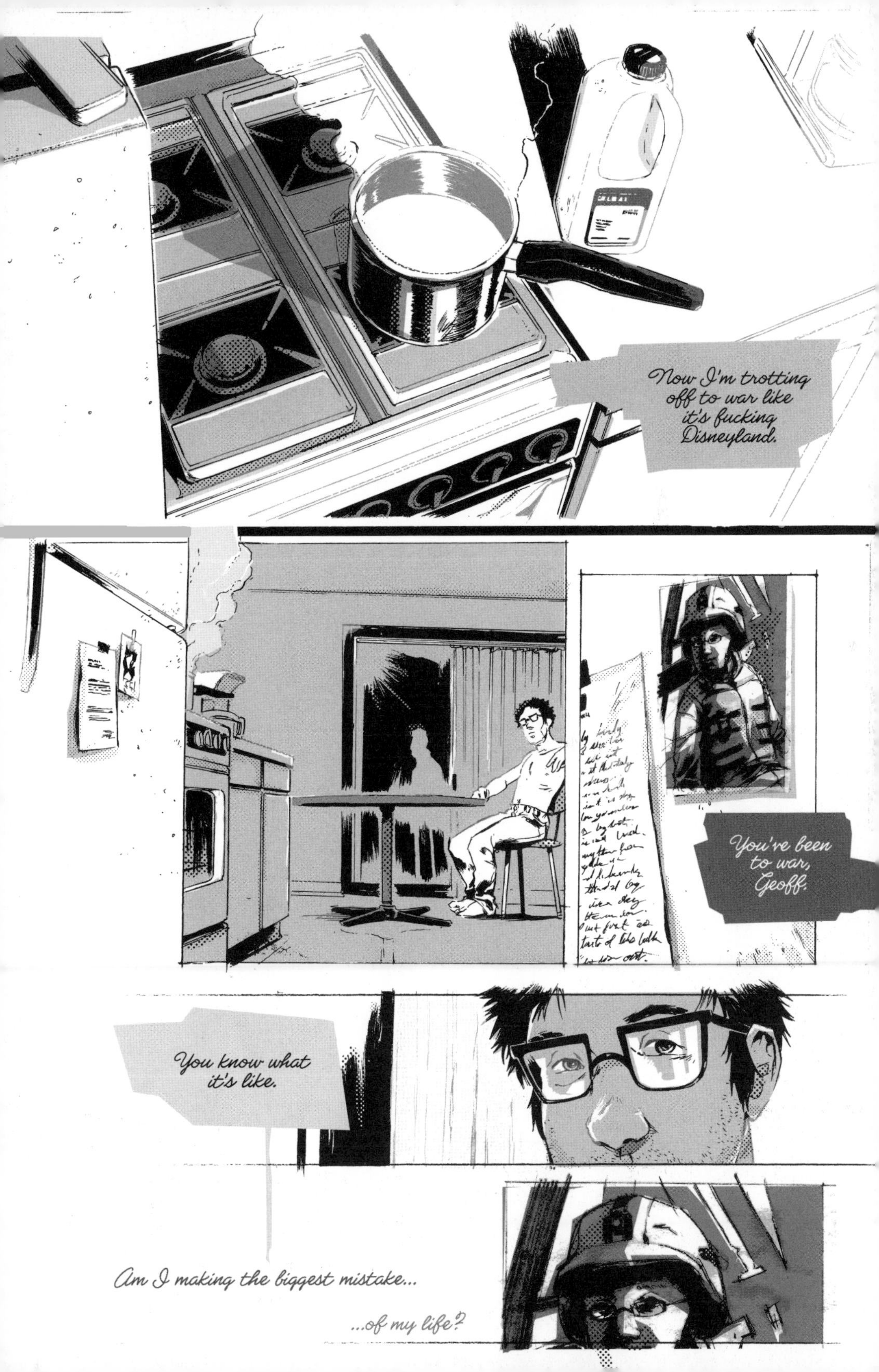
Now I'm trotting off to war like it's fucking Disneyland.
You've been to war, Geoff.
You know what it's like.
Am I making the biggest mistake...
...of my life?

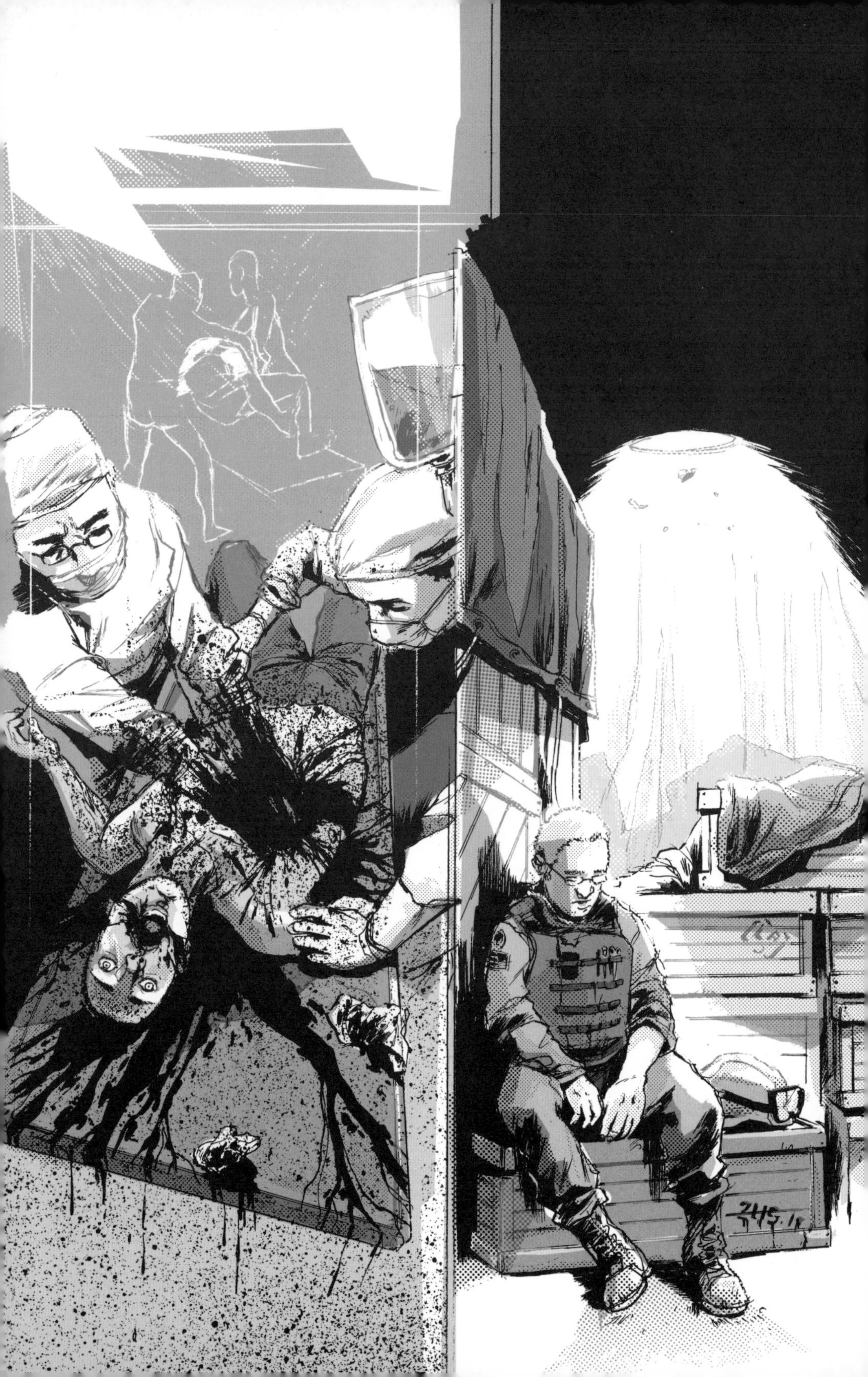

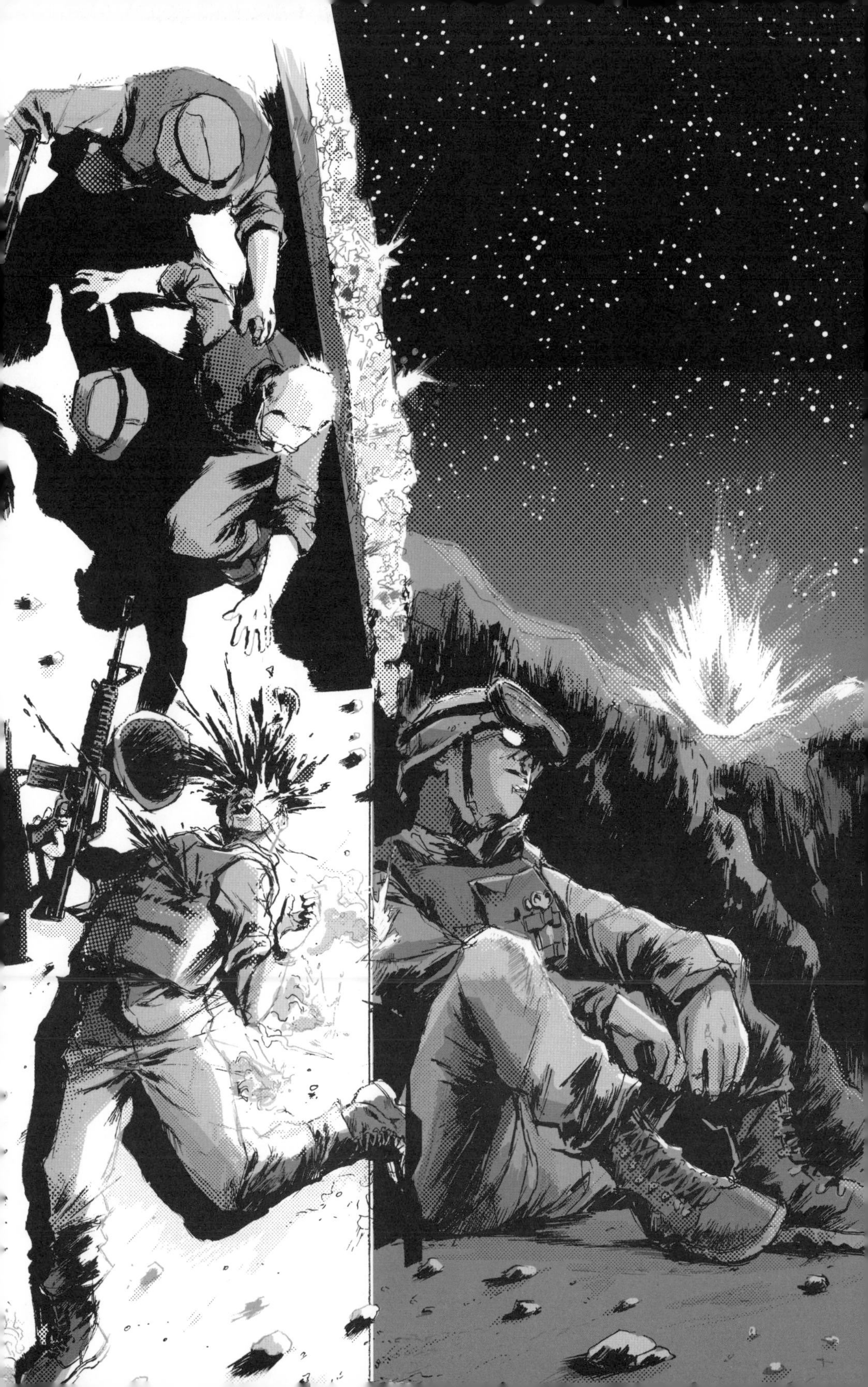

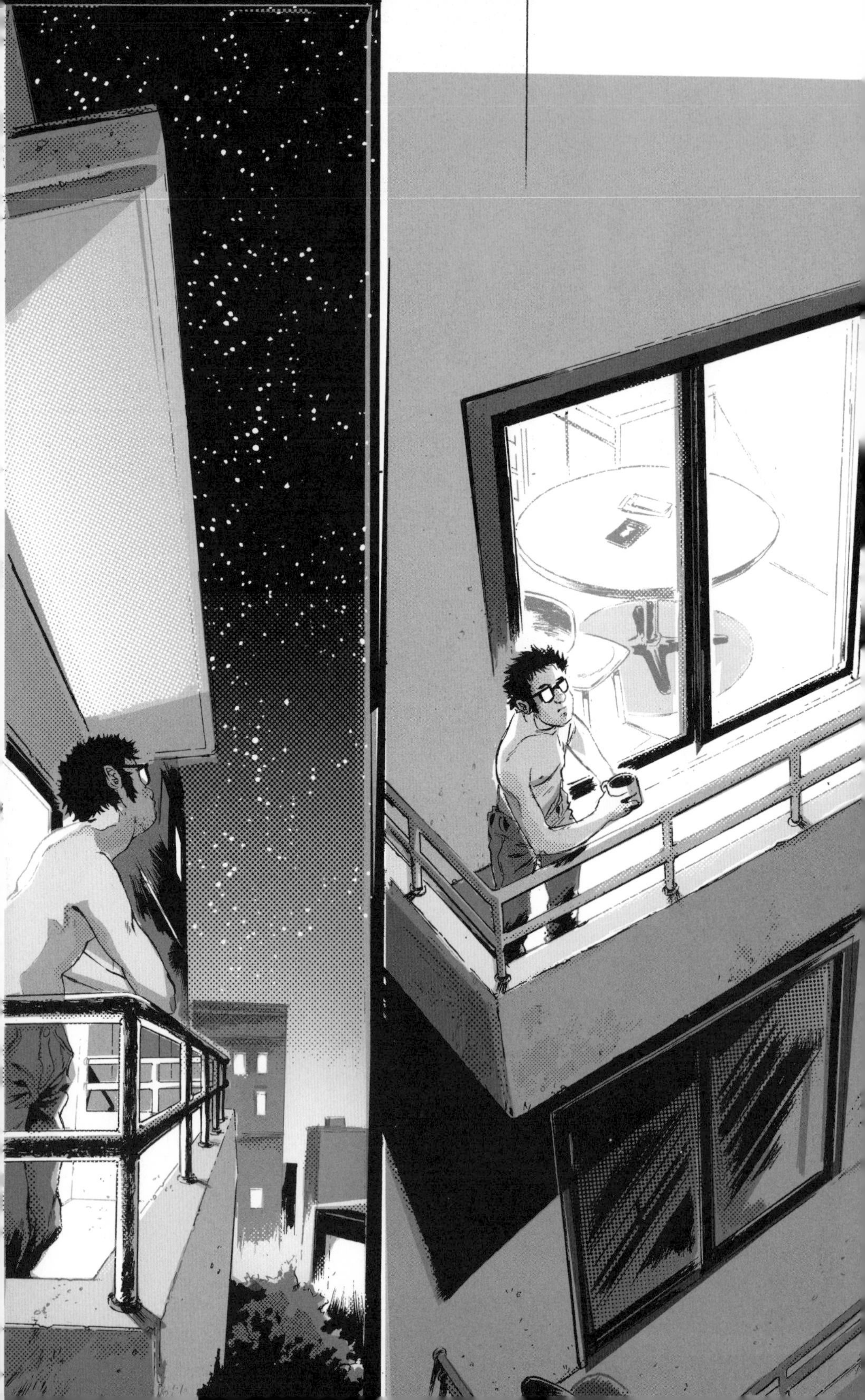

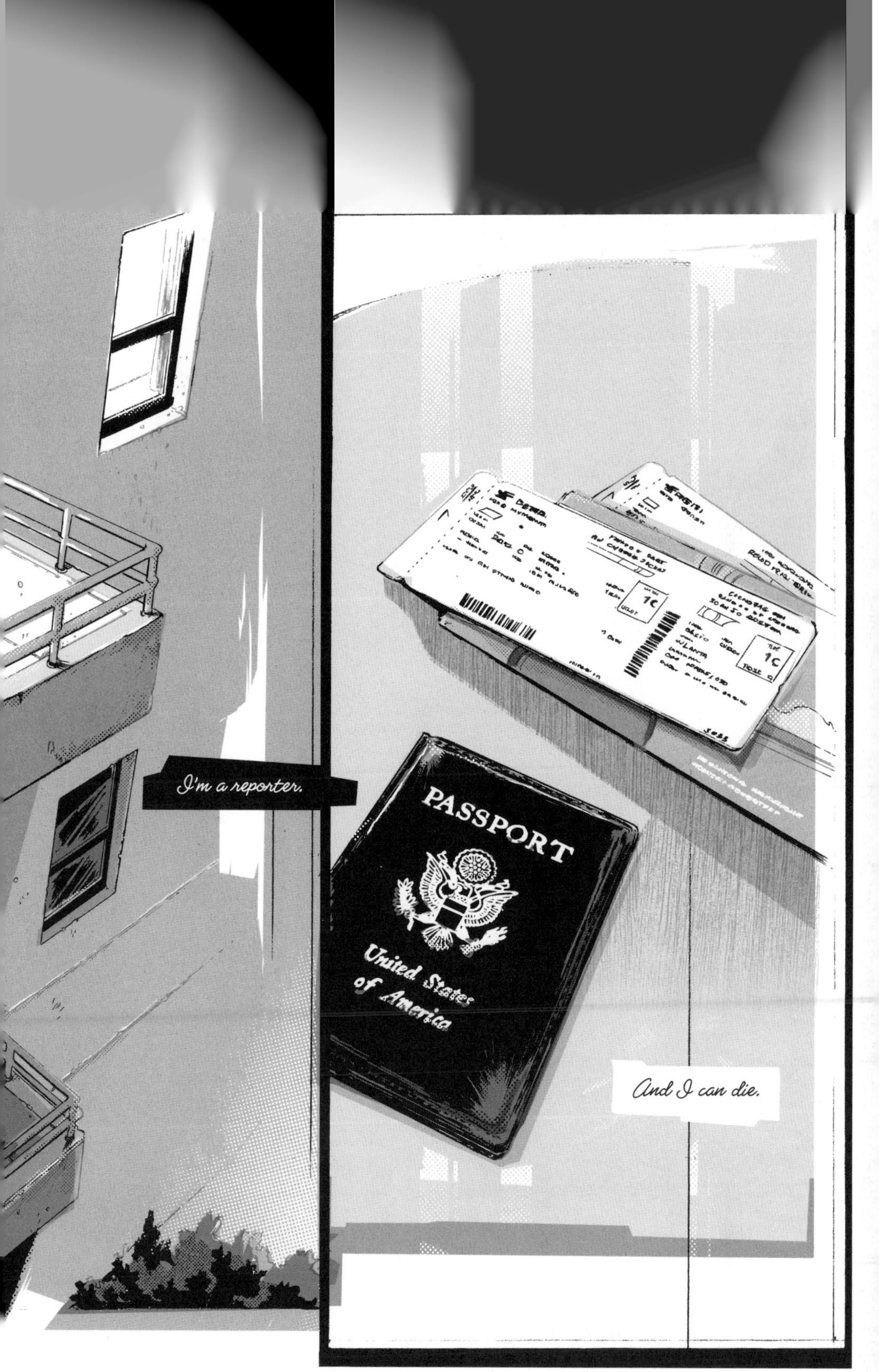
I'm a reporter.
PASSPORT
United States of America
And I can die.

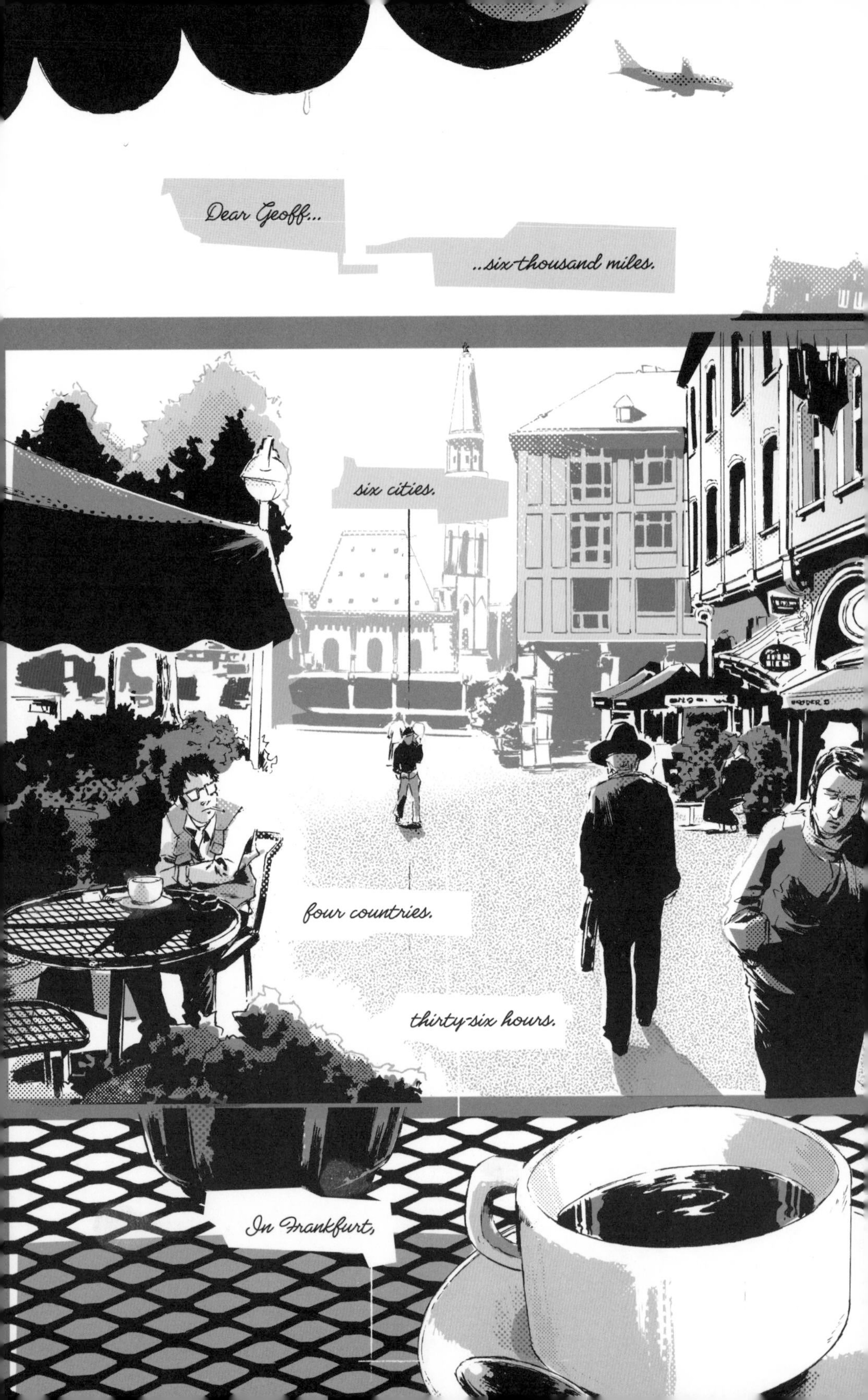
Dear Geoff...
..six thousand miles.
six cities.
four countries.
thirty-six hours.
In Frankfurt,

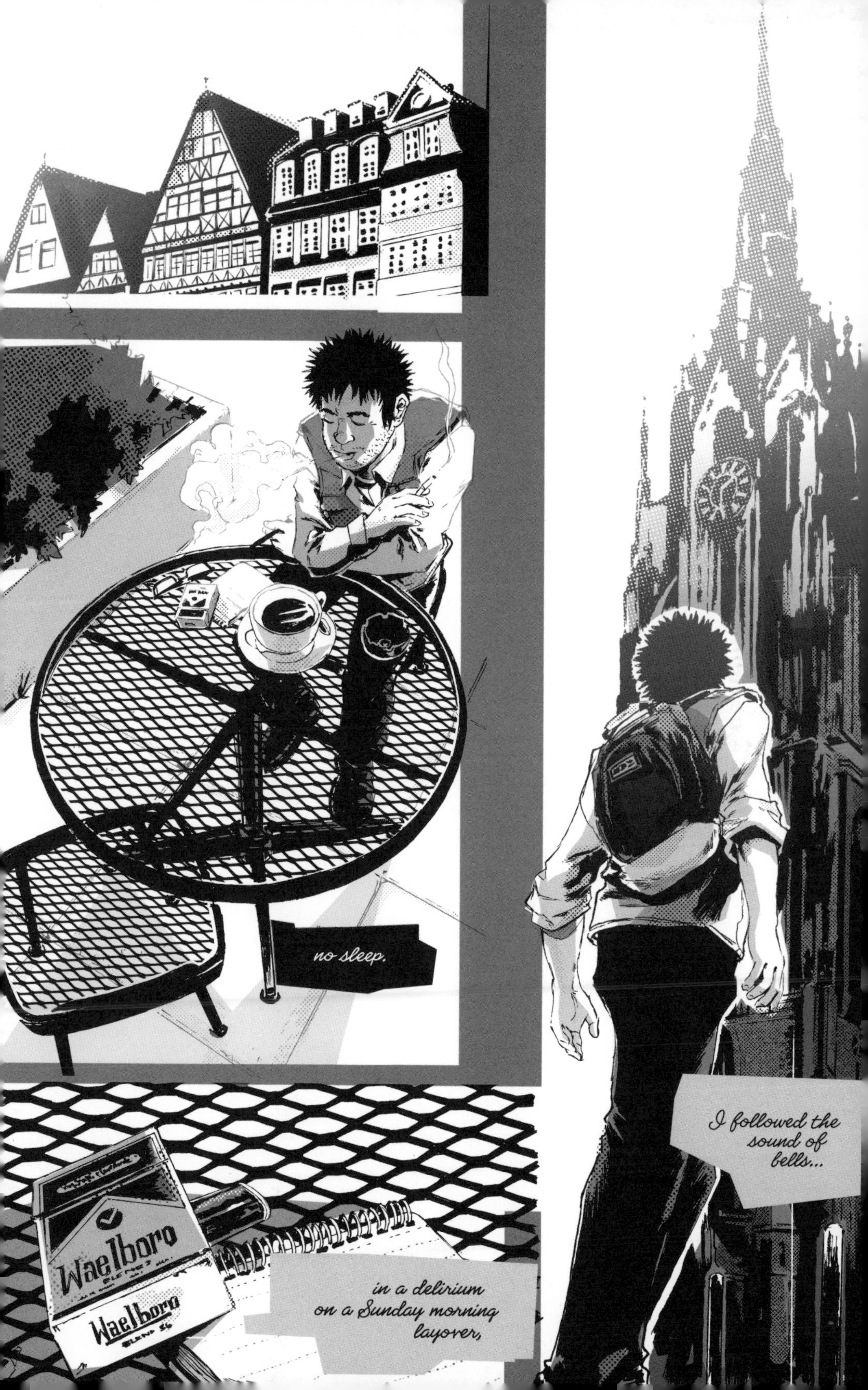
no sleep.
Waelboro
Waelboro
in a delirium on a Sunday morning layover,
I followed the sound of bells...

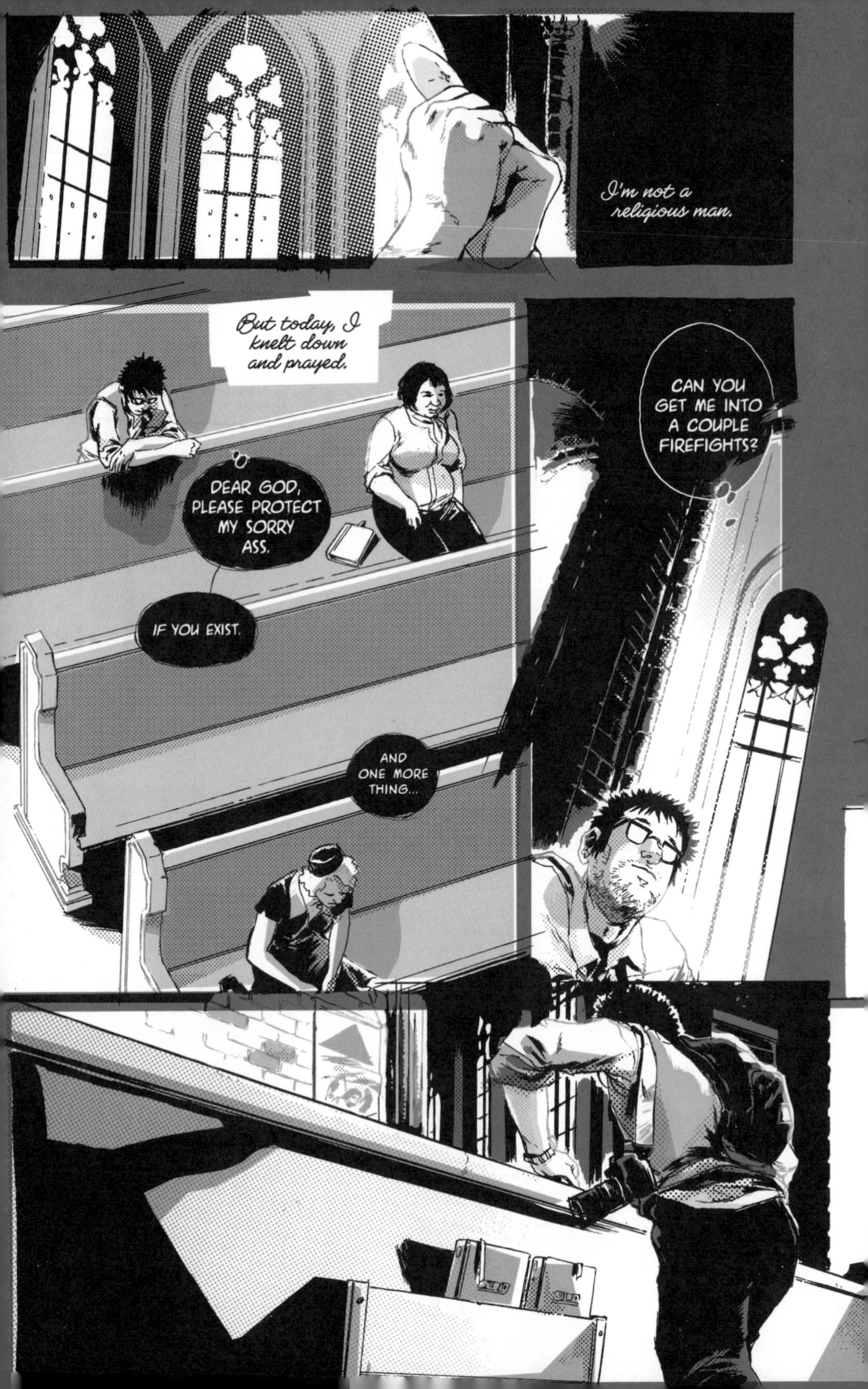
I'm not a religious man.
But today, I knelt down and prayed.
DEAR GOD, PLEASE PROTECT MY SORRY ASS.
IF YOU EXIST.
AND ONE MORE THING...
CAN YOU GET ME INTO A COUPLE FIREFIGHTS?

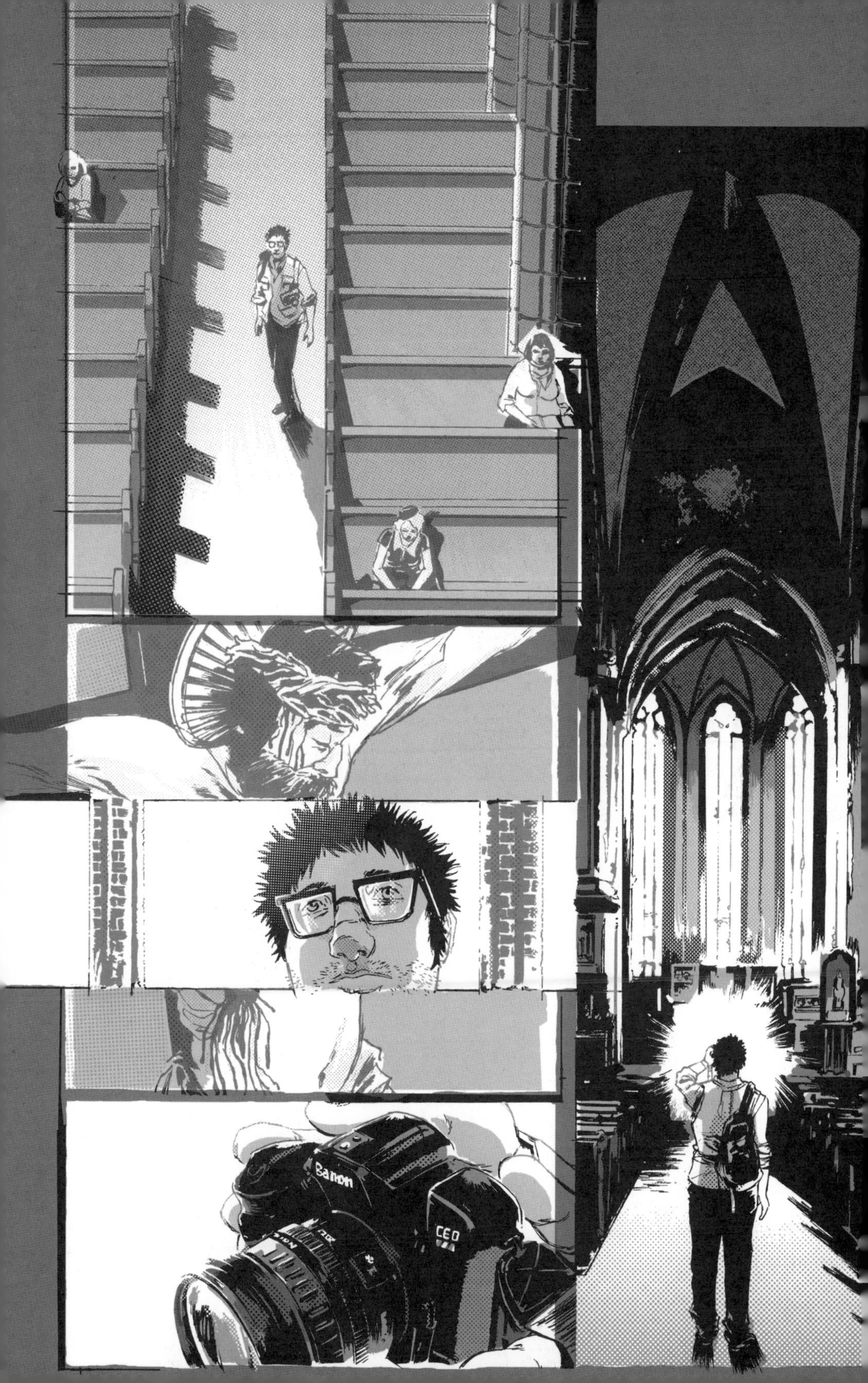
Banon
CEO

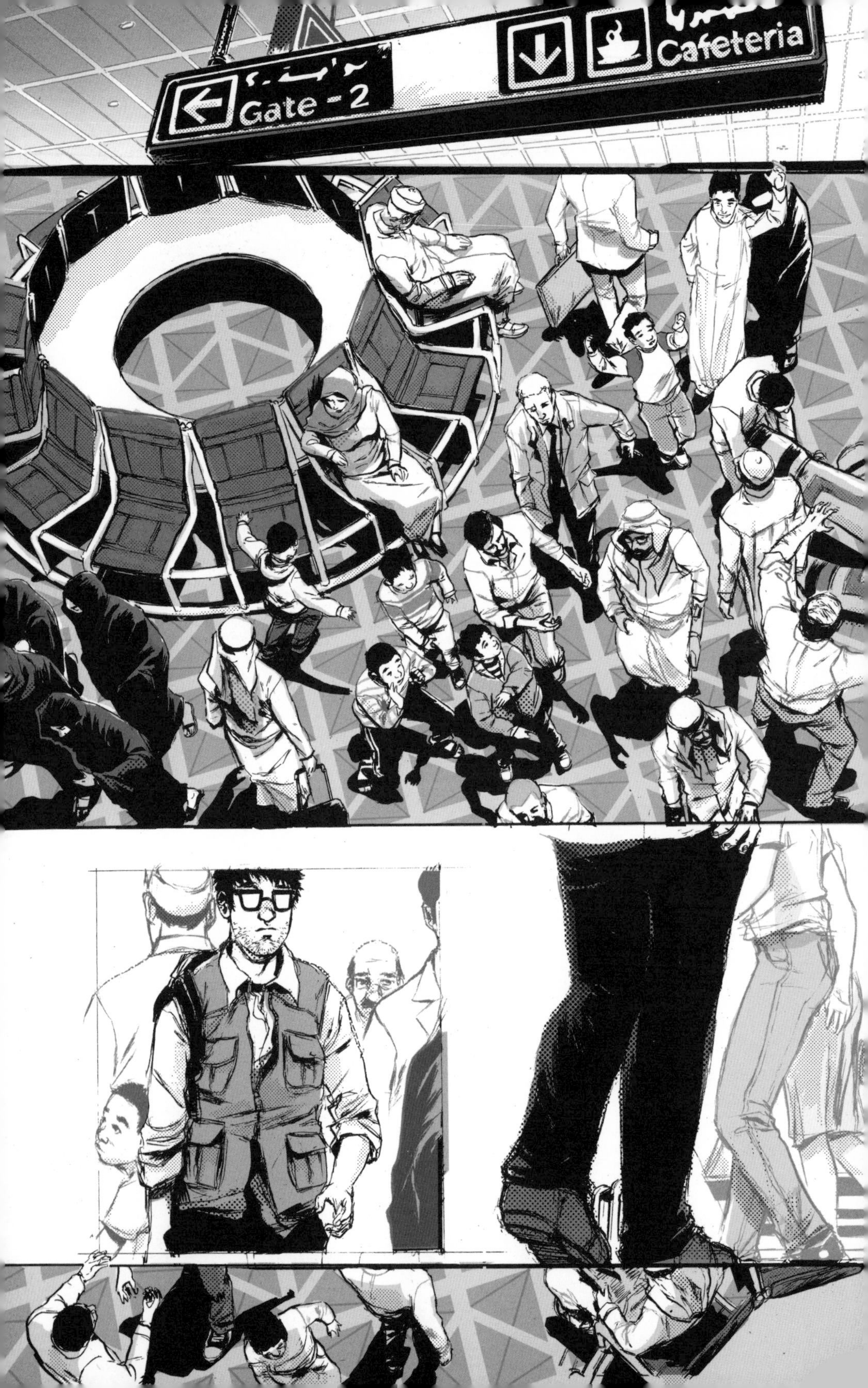
Gate - 2
Cafeteria

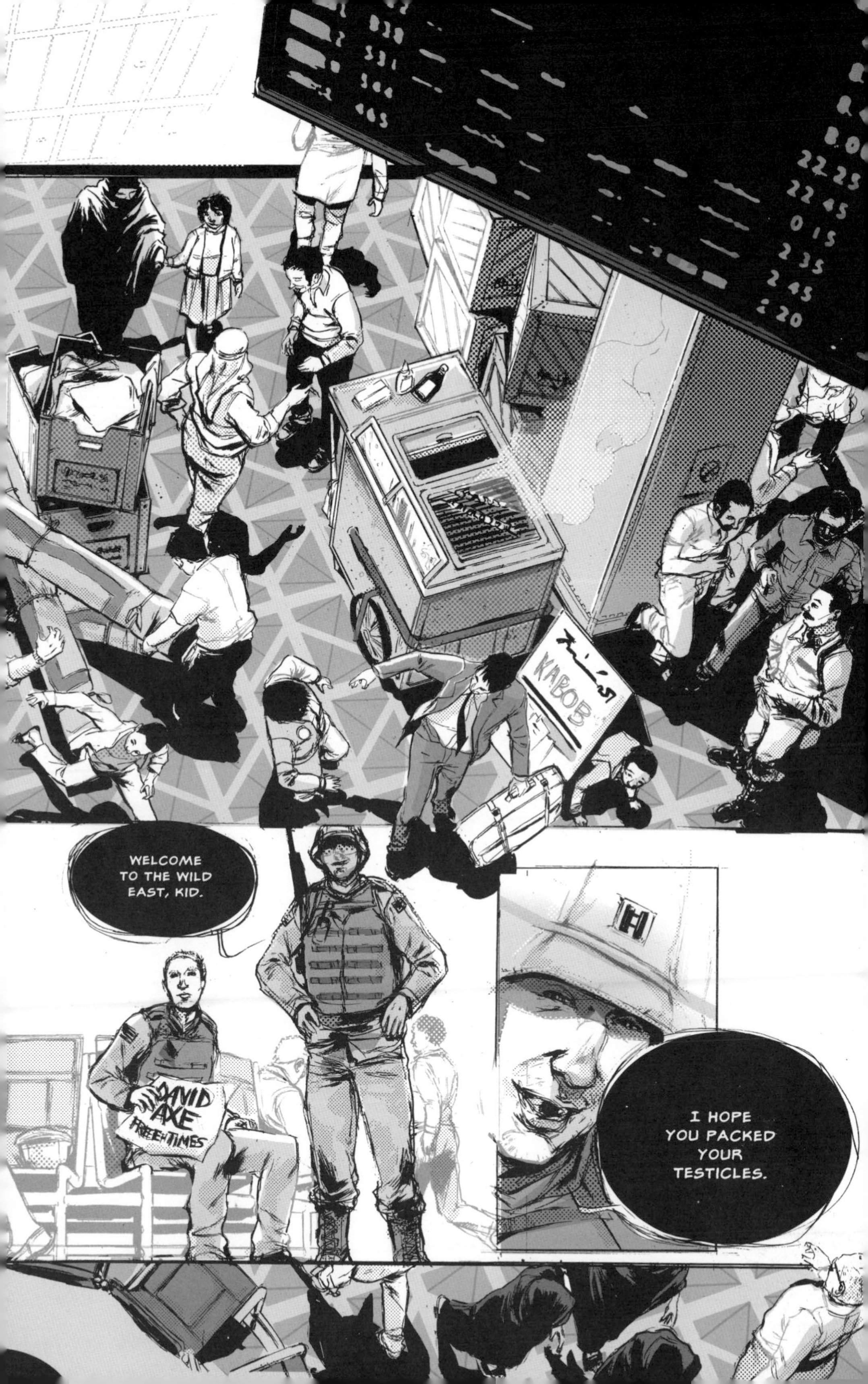
KABOB
WELCOME TO THE WILD EAST, KID.
DAVID AXE
I HOPE YOU PACKED YOUR TESTICLES.

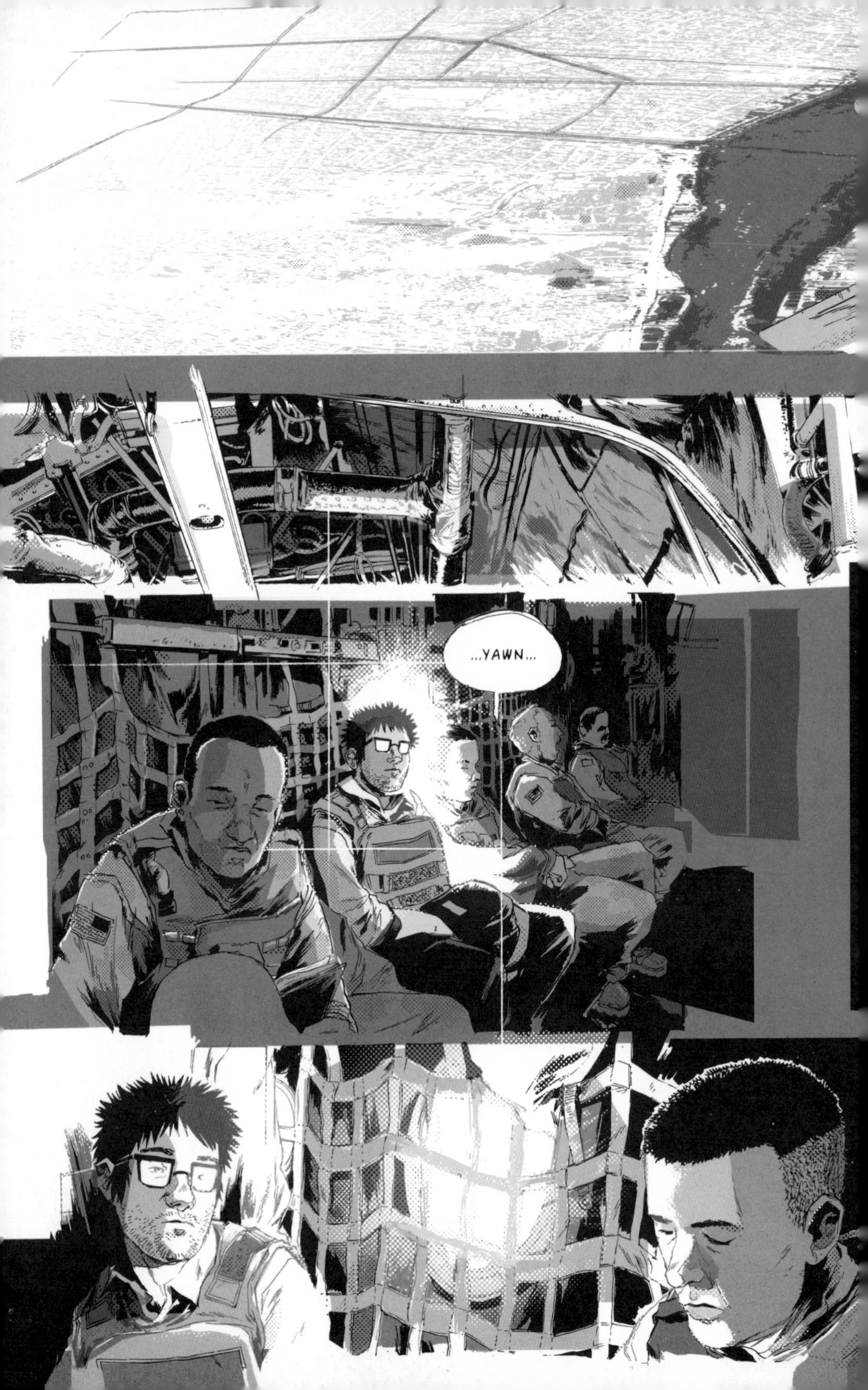
...YAWN...

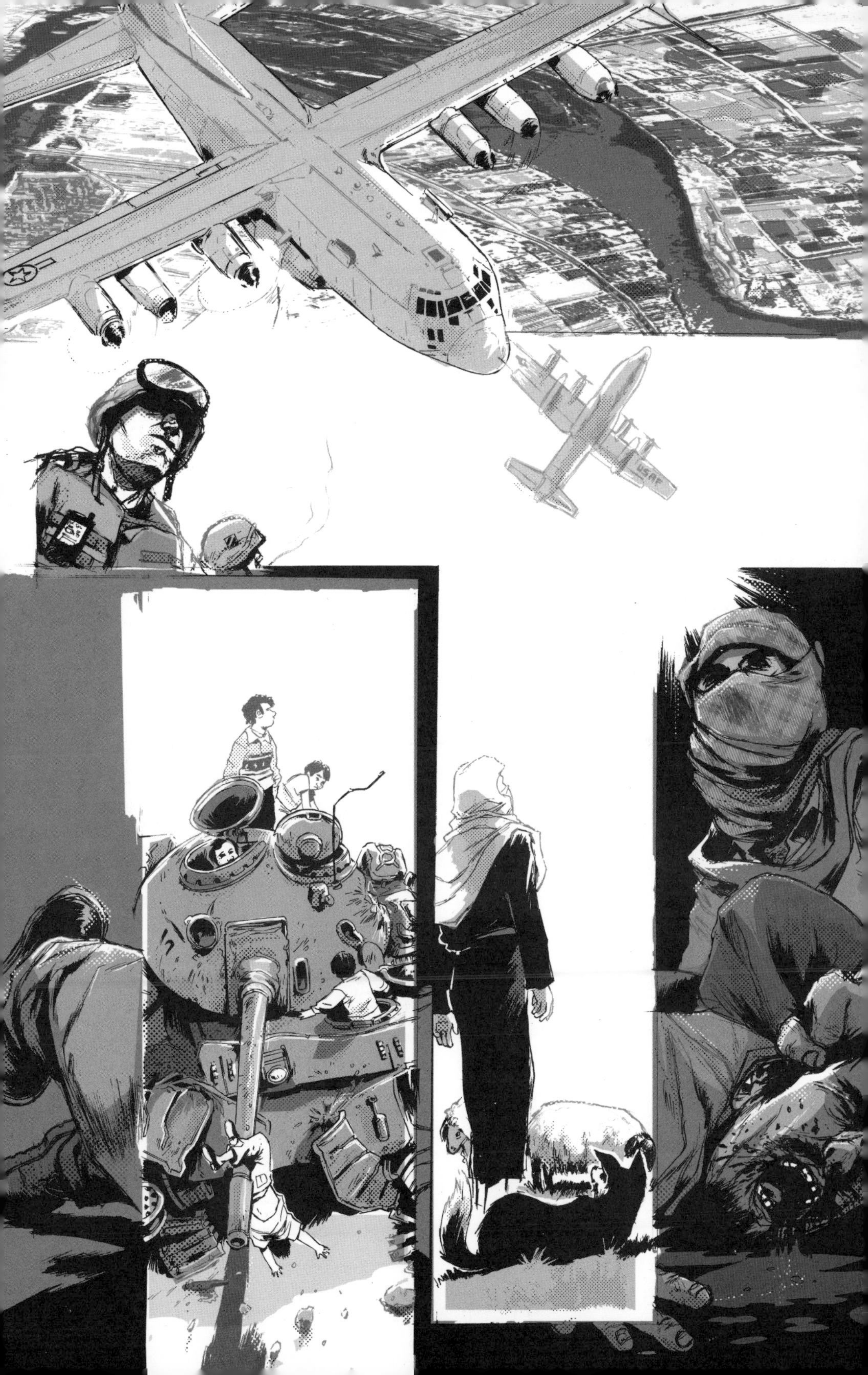
USAF

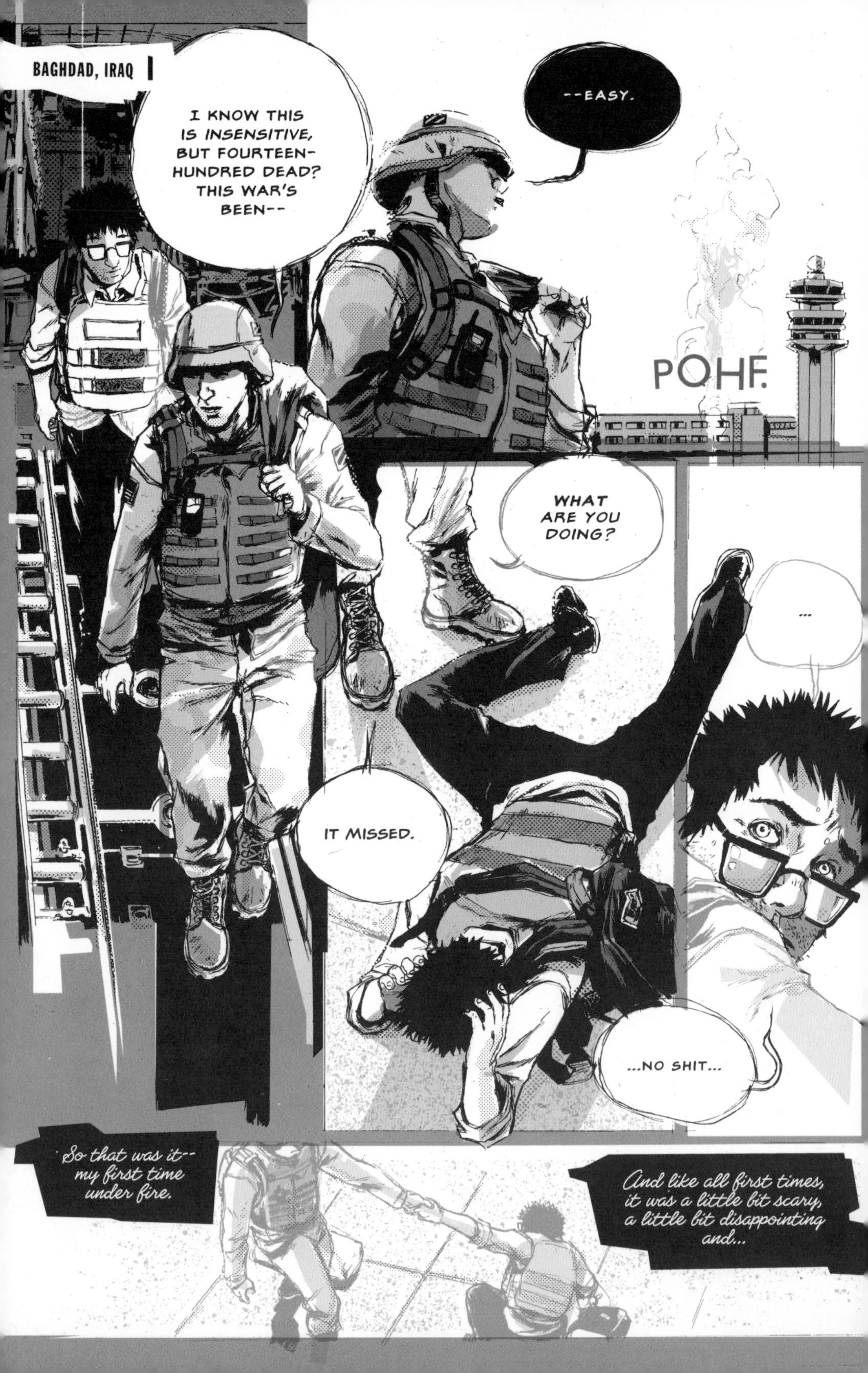
BAGHDAD, IRAQ
I KNOW THIS IS INSENSITIVE, BUT FOURTEEN-HUNDRED DEAD? THIS WAR'S BEEN--
--EASY.
POHF.
WHAT ARE YOU DOING?
IT MISSED.
...
...NO SHIT...
So that was it--my first time under fire.
And like all first times, it was a little bit scary, a little bit disappointing and...

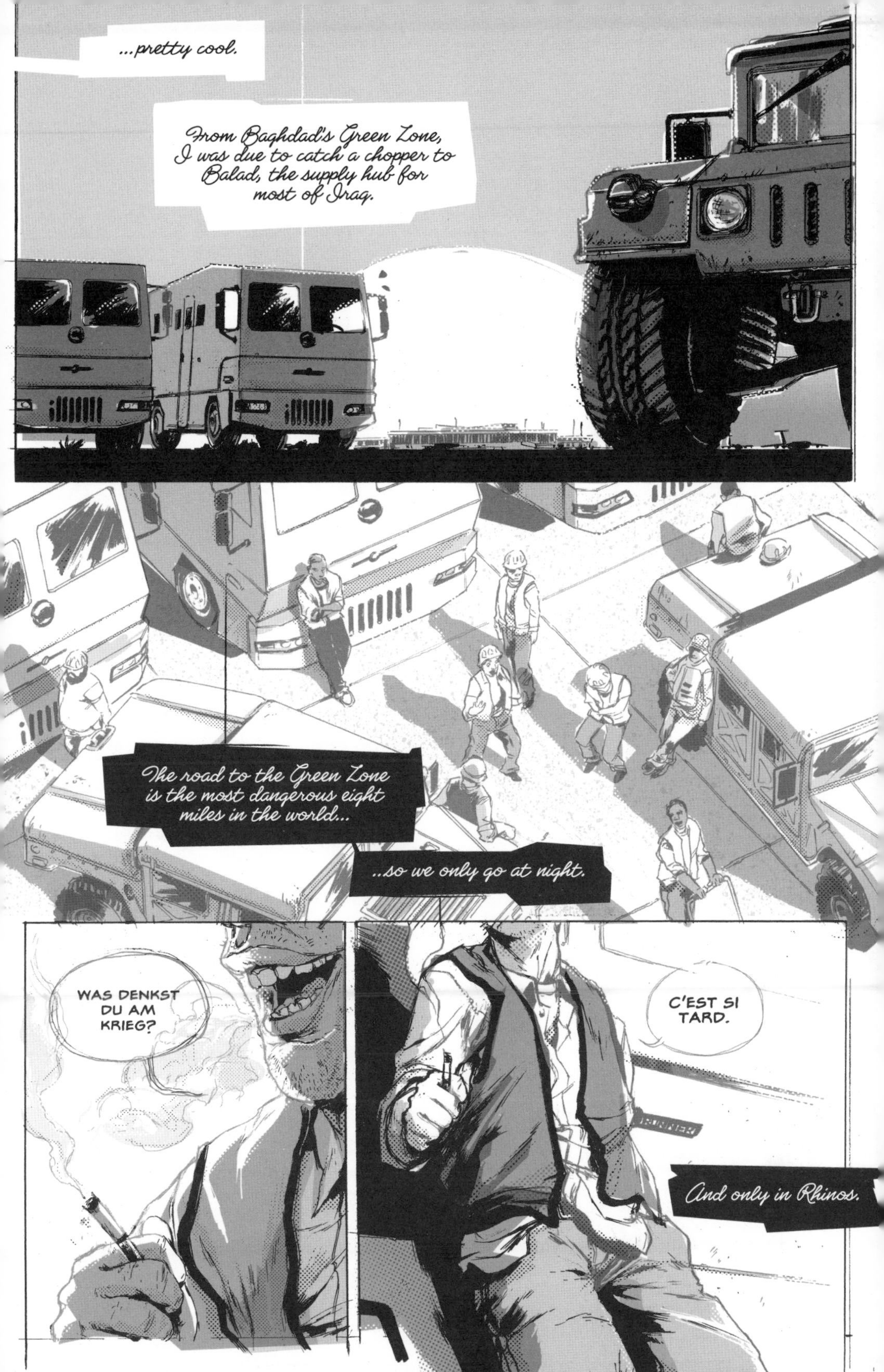

...pretty cool.
From Baghdad's Green Zone, I was due to catch a chopper to Balad, the supply hub for most of Iraq.
The road to the Green Zone is the most dangerous eight miles in the world...
..so we only go at night.
WAS DENKST DU AM KRIEG?
C'EST SI TARD.
And only in Rhinos.

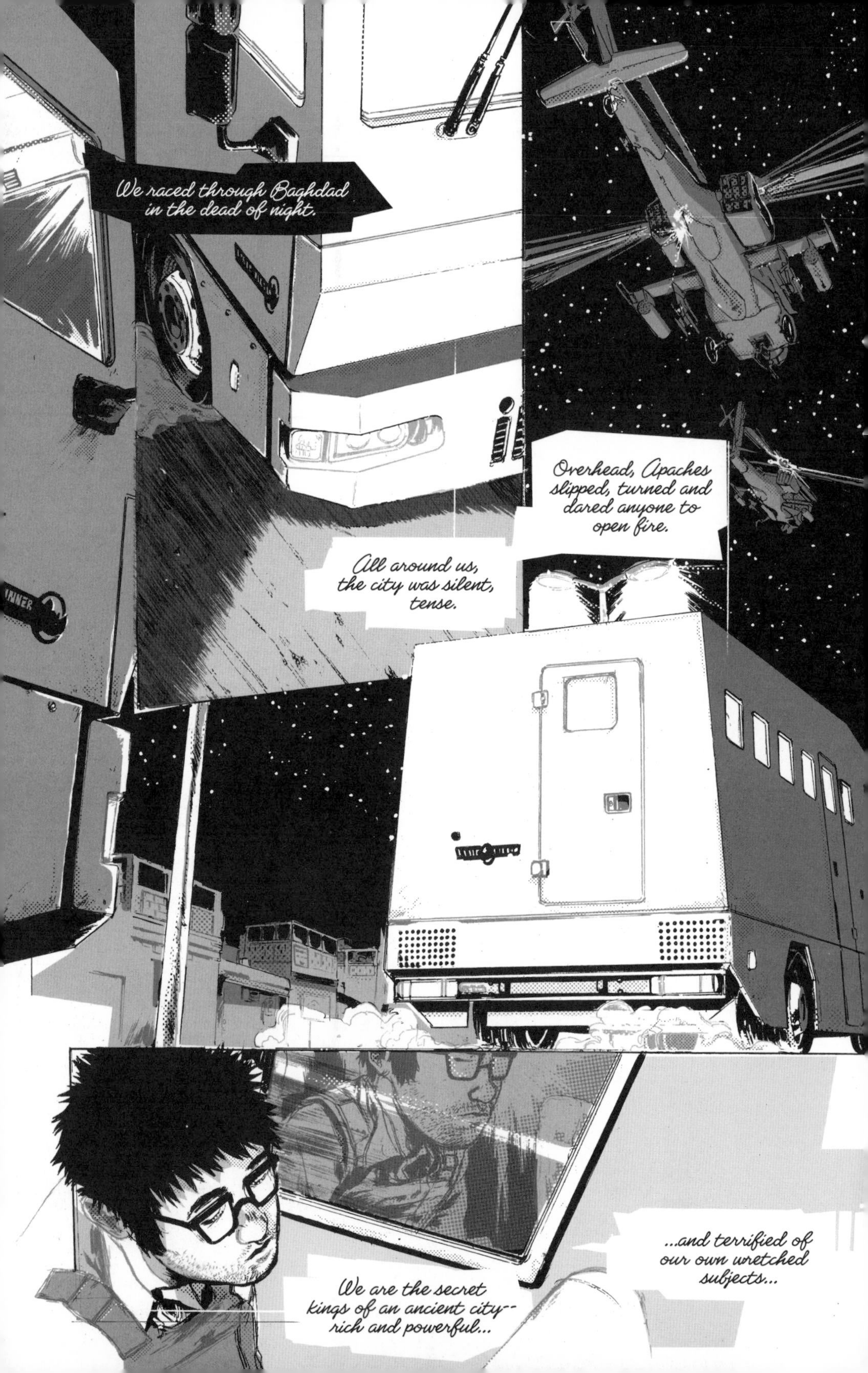
We raced through Baghdad in the dead of night.
Overhead, Apaches slipped, turned and dared anyone to open fire.
All around us, the city was silent, tense.
We are the secret kings of an ancient city--rich and powerful...
...and terrified of our own wretched subjects...

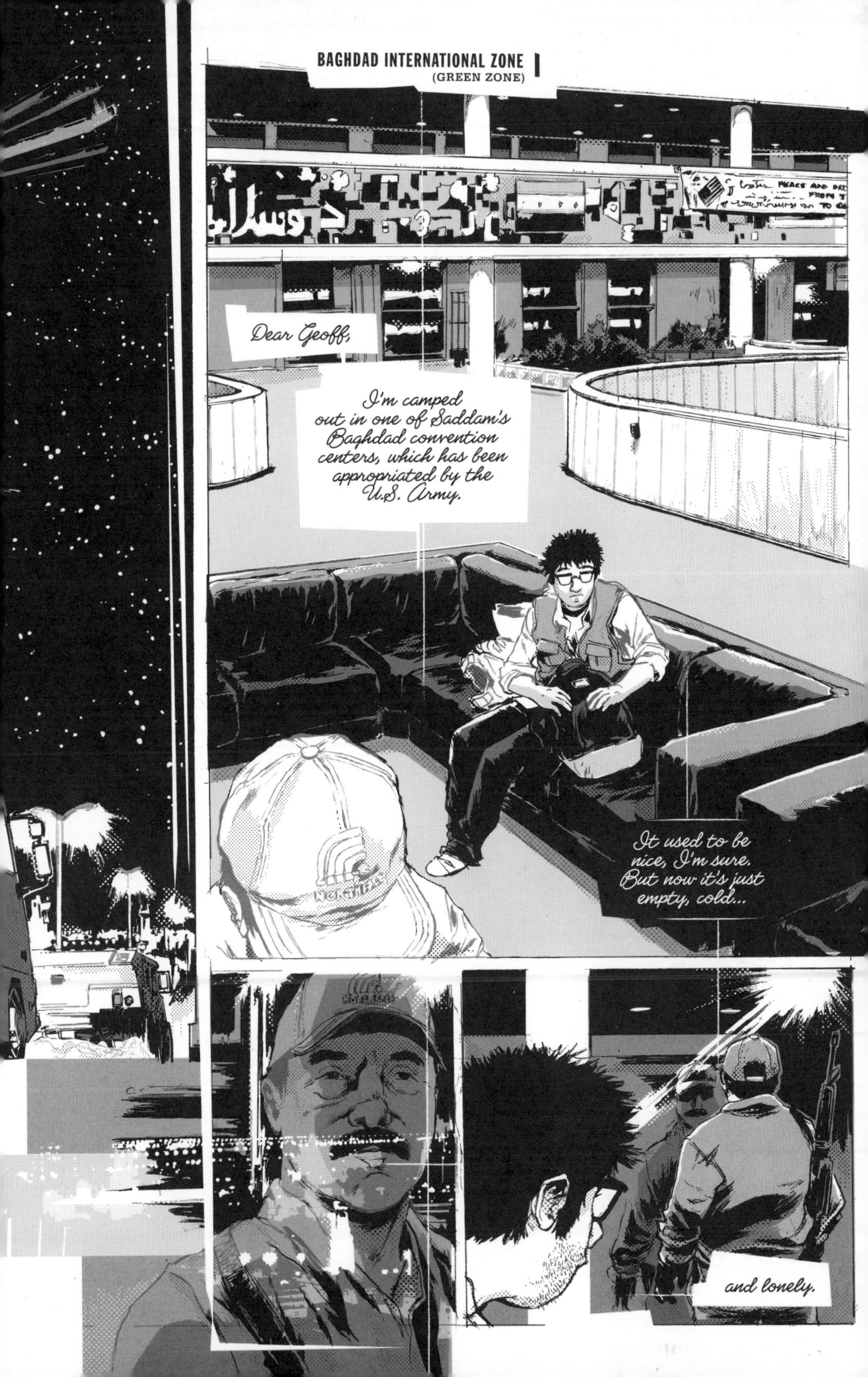
BAGHDAD INTERNATIONAL ZONE
(GREEN ZONE)
Dear Geoff,
I'm camped out in one of Saddam's Baghdad convention centers, which has been appropriated by the U.S. Army.
It used to be nice, I'm sure. But now it's just empty, cold...
and lonely.

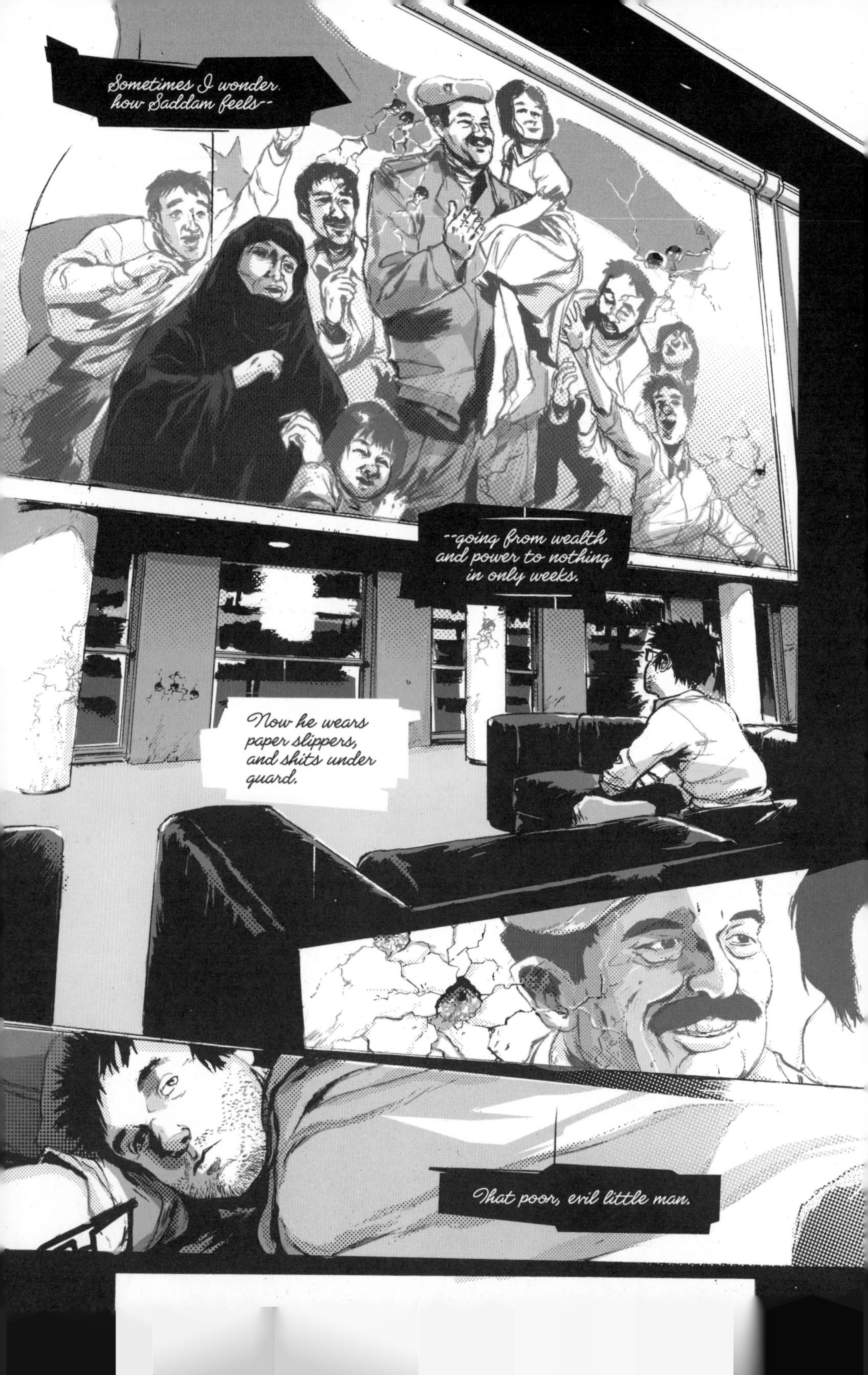
Sometimes I wonder how Saddam feels--
--going from wealth and power to nothing in only weeks.
Now he wears paper slippers, and shits under guard.
That poor, evil little man.

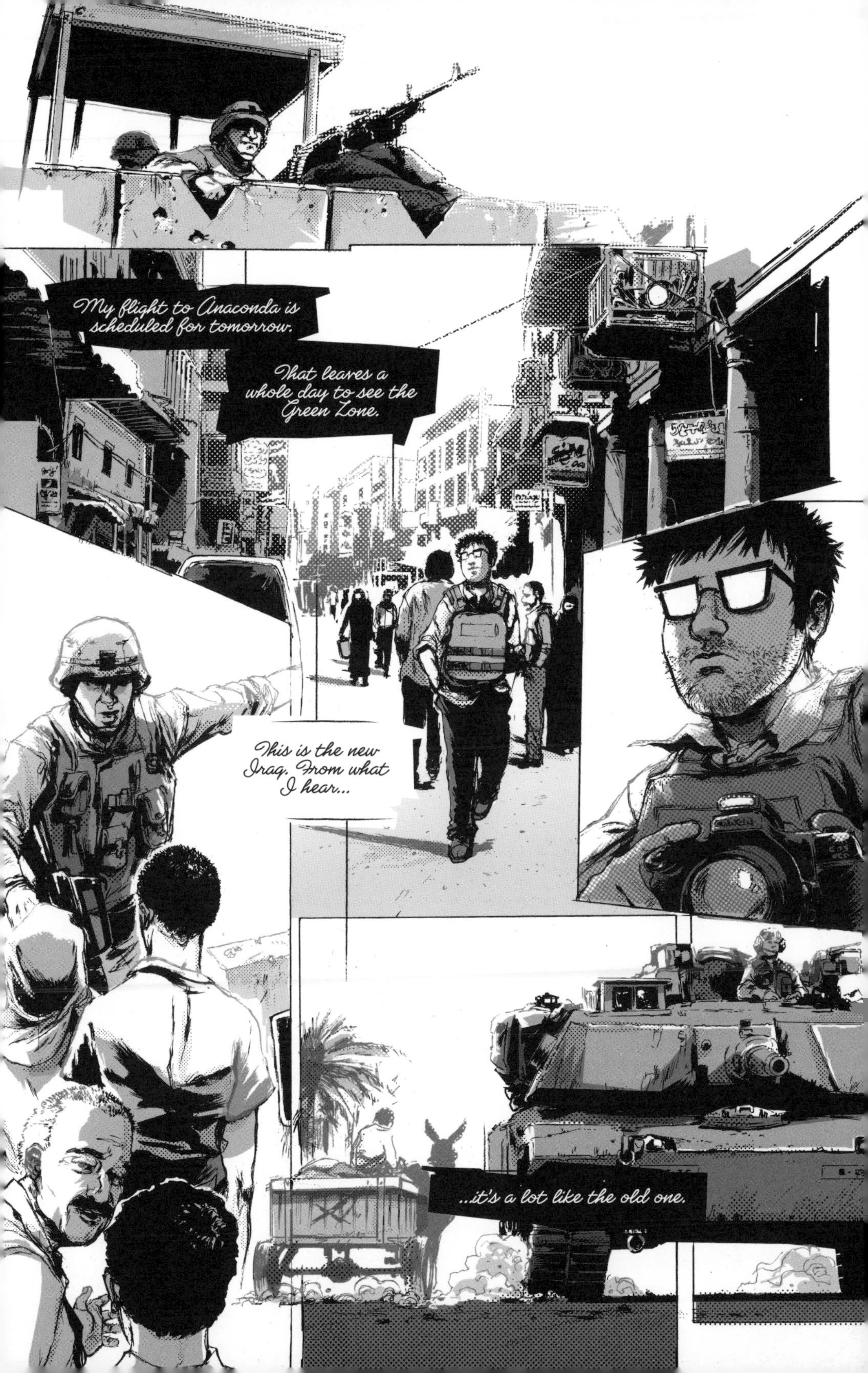
My flight to Anaconda is scheduled for tomorrow.
That leaves a whole day to see the Green Zone.
This is the new Iraq. From what I hear...
...it's a lot like the old one.

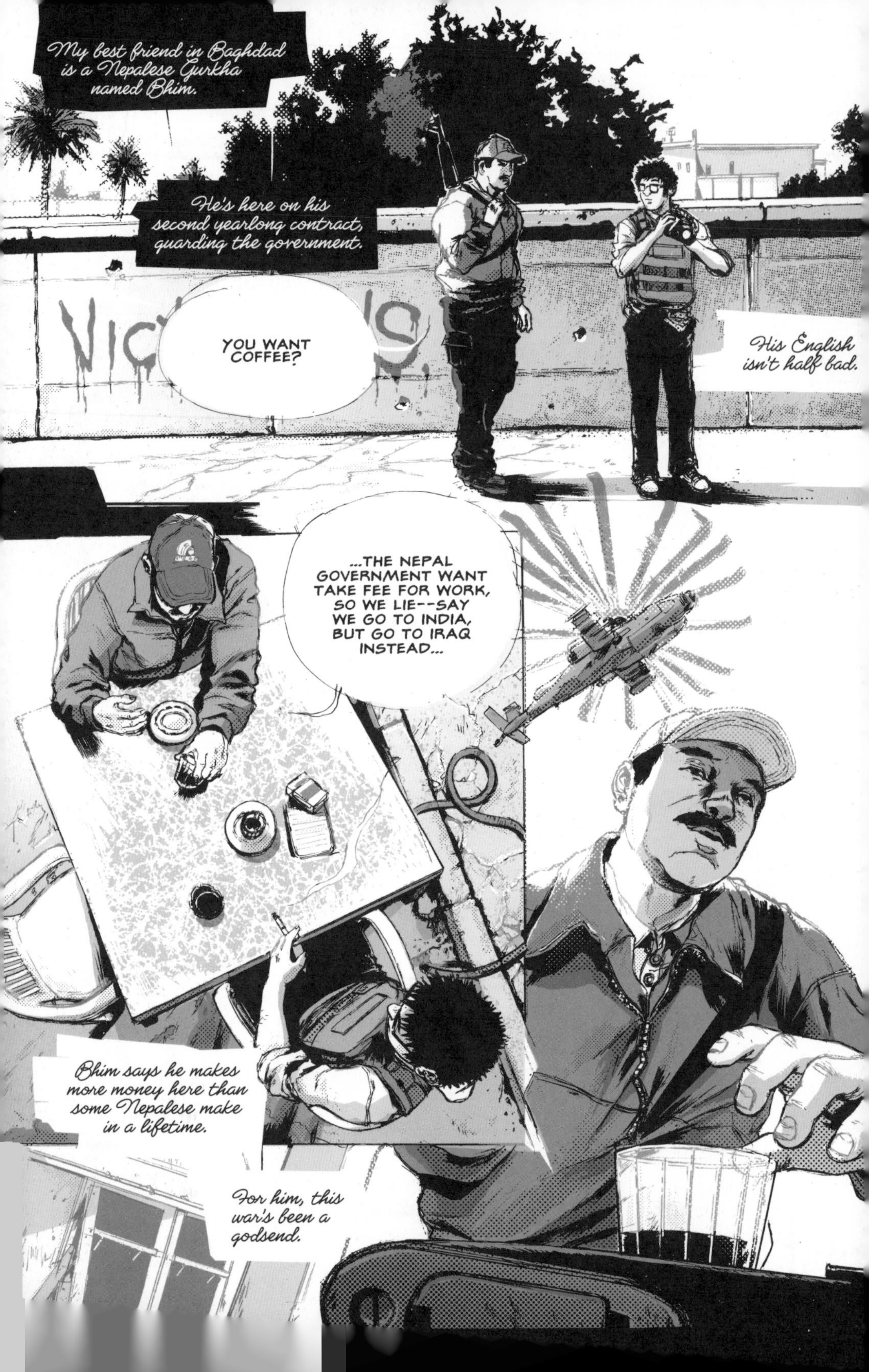
My best friend in Baghdad is a Nepalese Gurkha named Bhim.
He's here on his second yearlong contract, guarding the government.
YOU WANT COFFEE?
His English isn't half bad.
...THE NEPAL GOVERNMENT WANT TAKE FEE FOR WORK, SO WE LIE--SAY WE GO TO INDIA, BUT GO TO IRAQ INSTEAD...
Bhim says he makes more money here than some Nepalese make in a lifetime.
For him, this war's been a godsend.

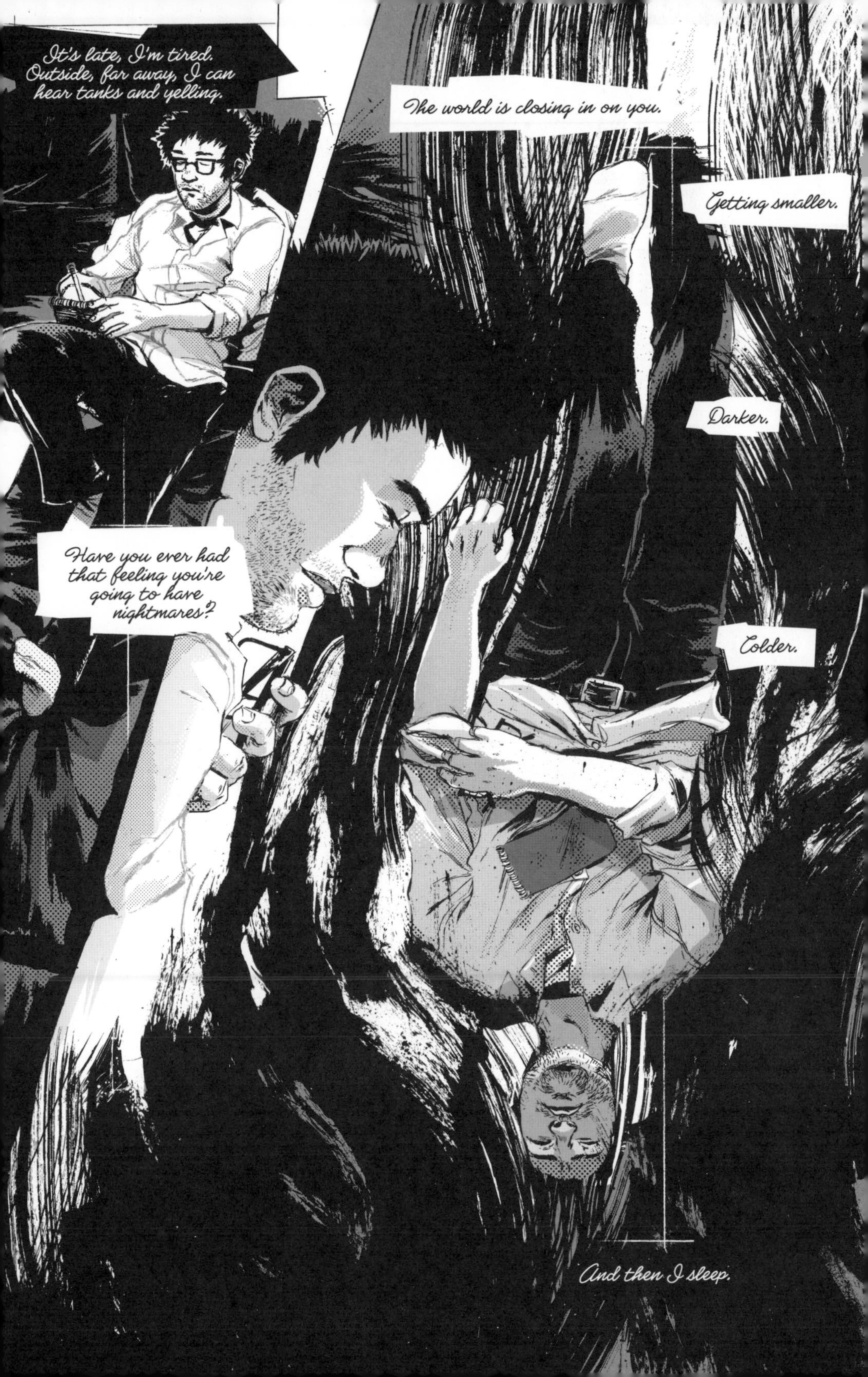
It's late, I'm tired. Outside, far away, I can hear tanks and yelling.
The world is closing in on you.
Getting smaller.
Darker.
Have you ever had that feeling you're going to have nightmares?
Colder.
And then I sleep.

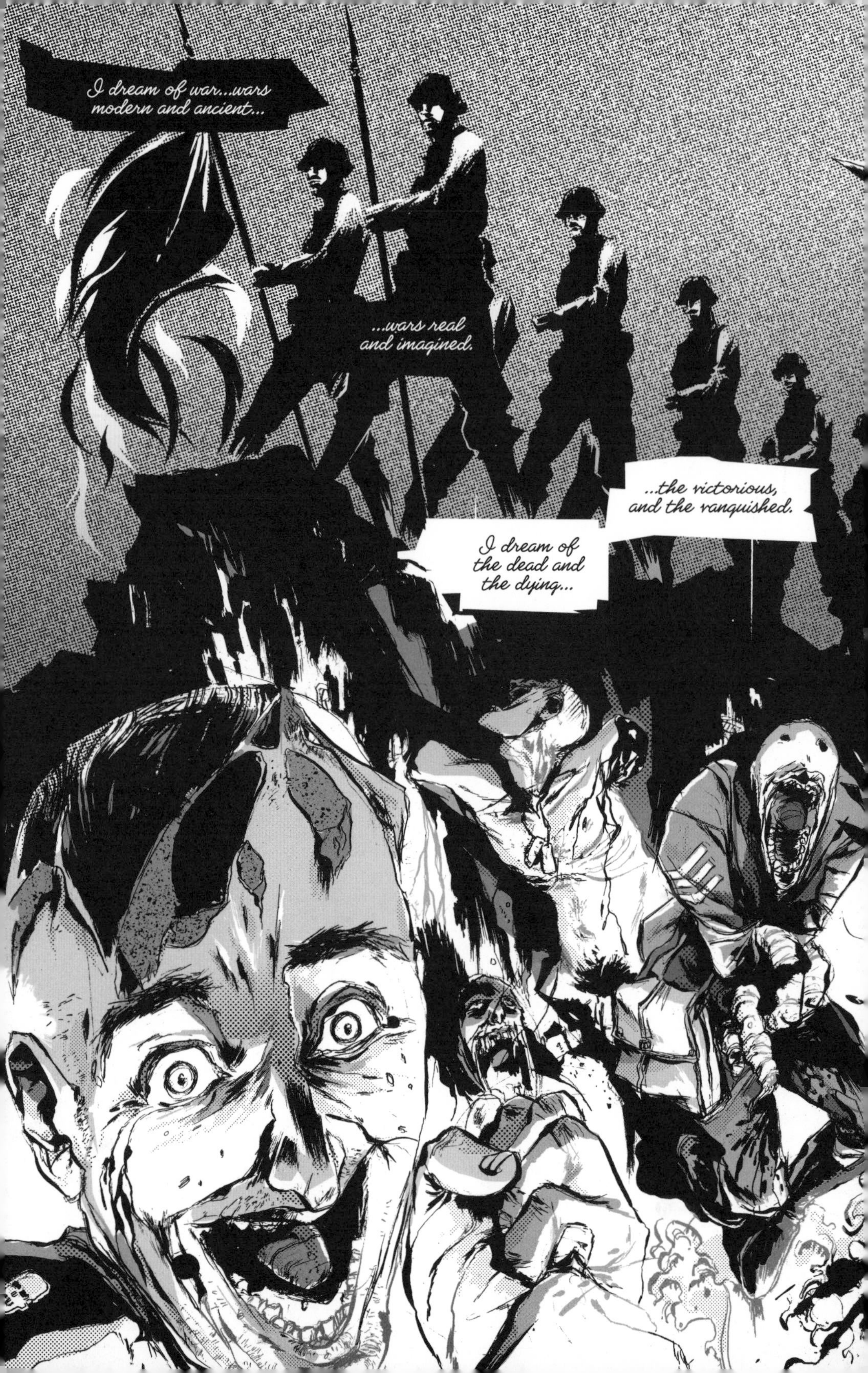
I dream of war...wars modern and ancient...
...wars real and imagined.
I dream of the dead and the dying...
...the victorious, and the vanquished.

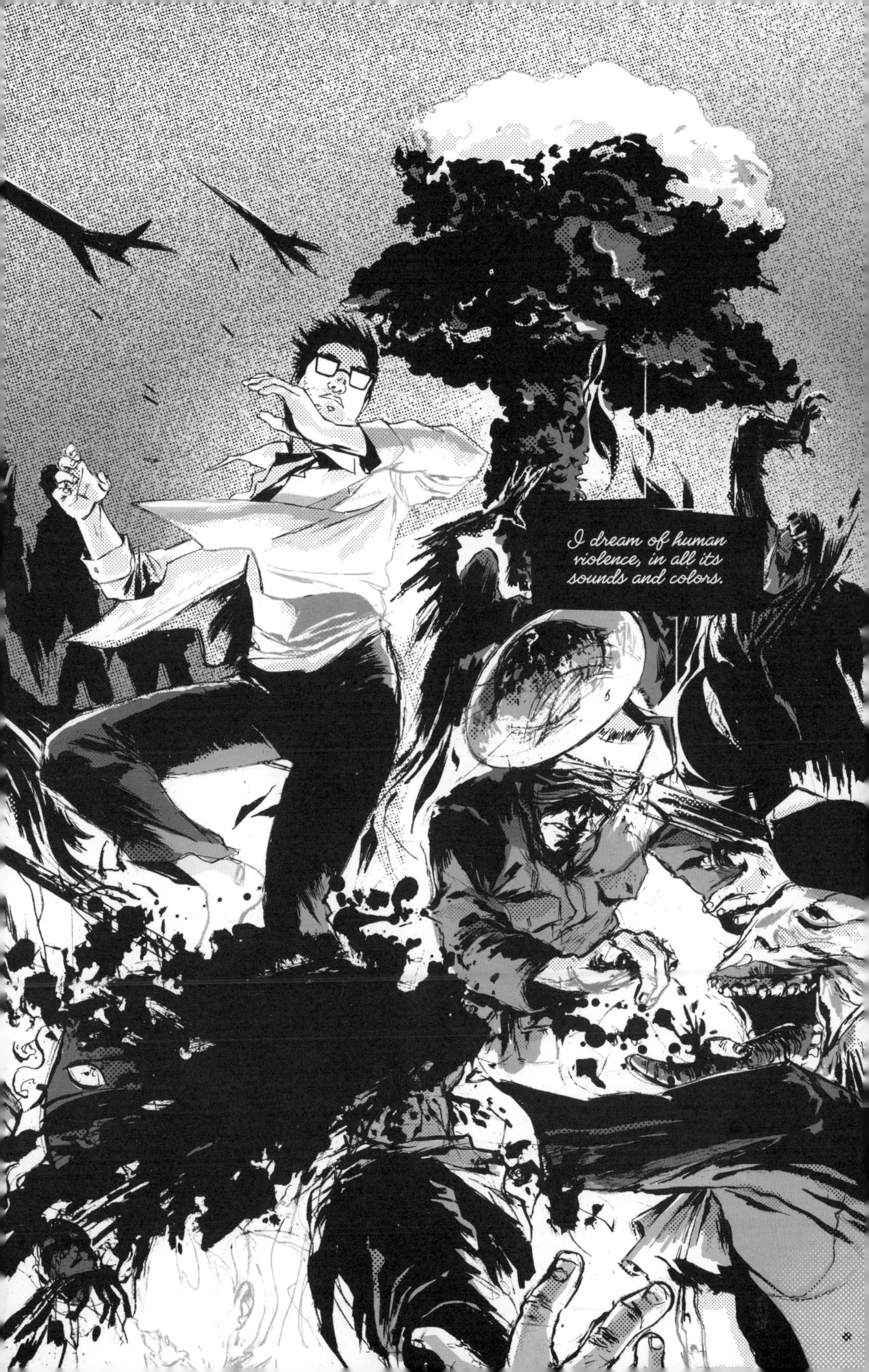
I dream of human violence, in all its sounds and colors.

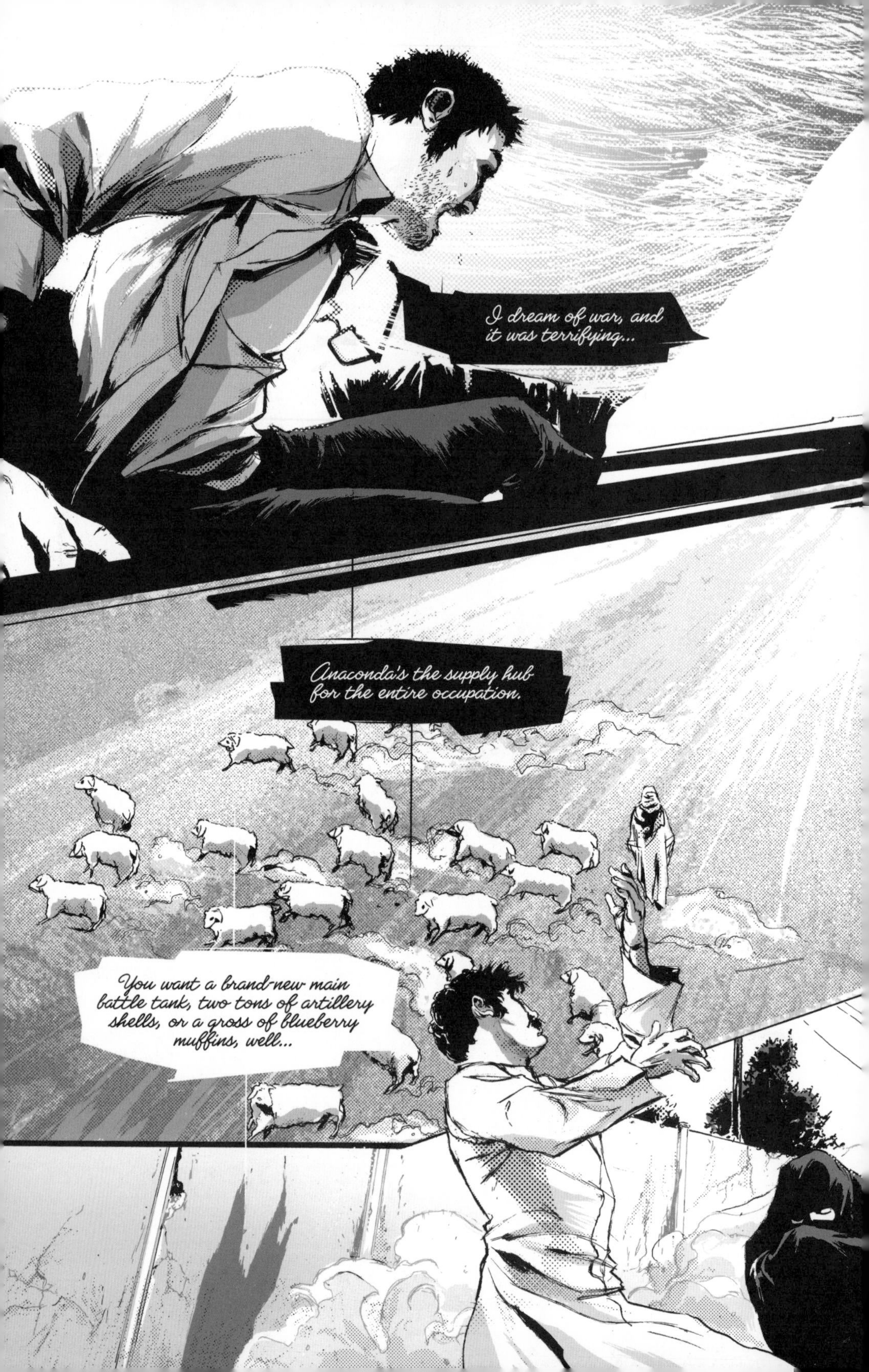
I dream of war, and it was terrifying...
Anaconda's the supply hub for the entire occupation.
You want a brand-new main battle tank, two tons of artillery shells, or a gross of blueberry muffins, well...

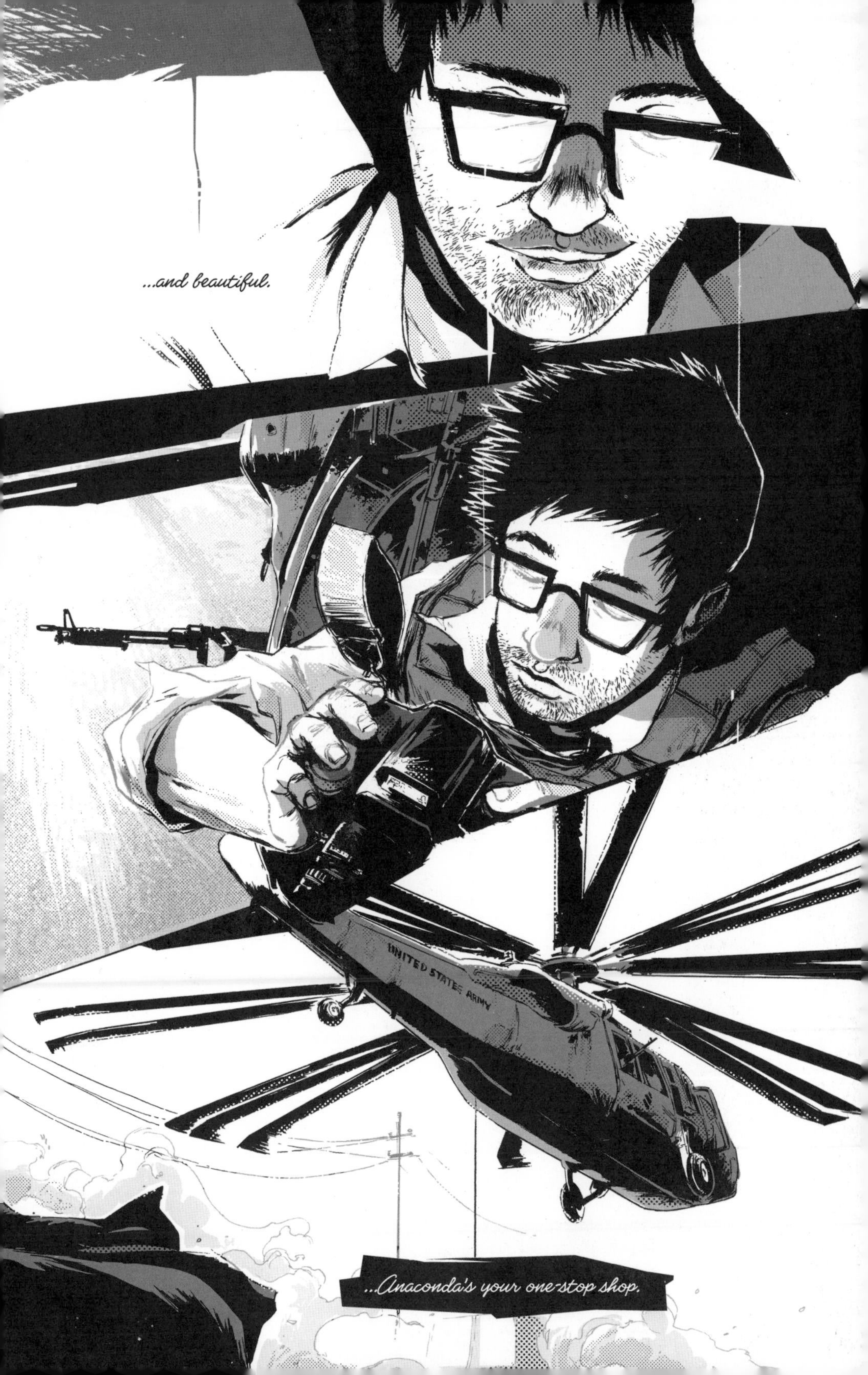
...and beautiful.
UNITED STATES ARMY
...Anaconda's your one-stop shop.

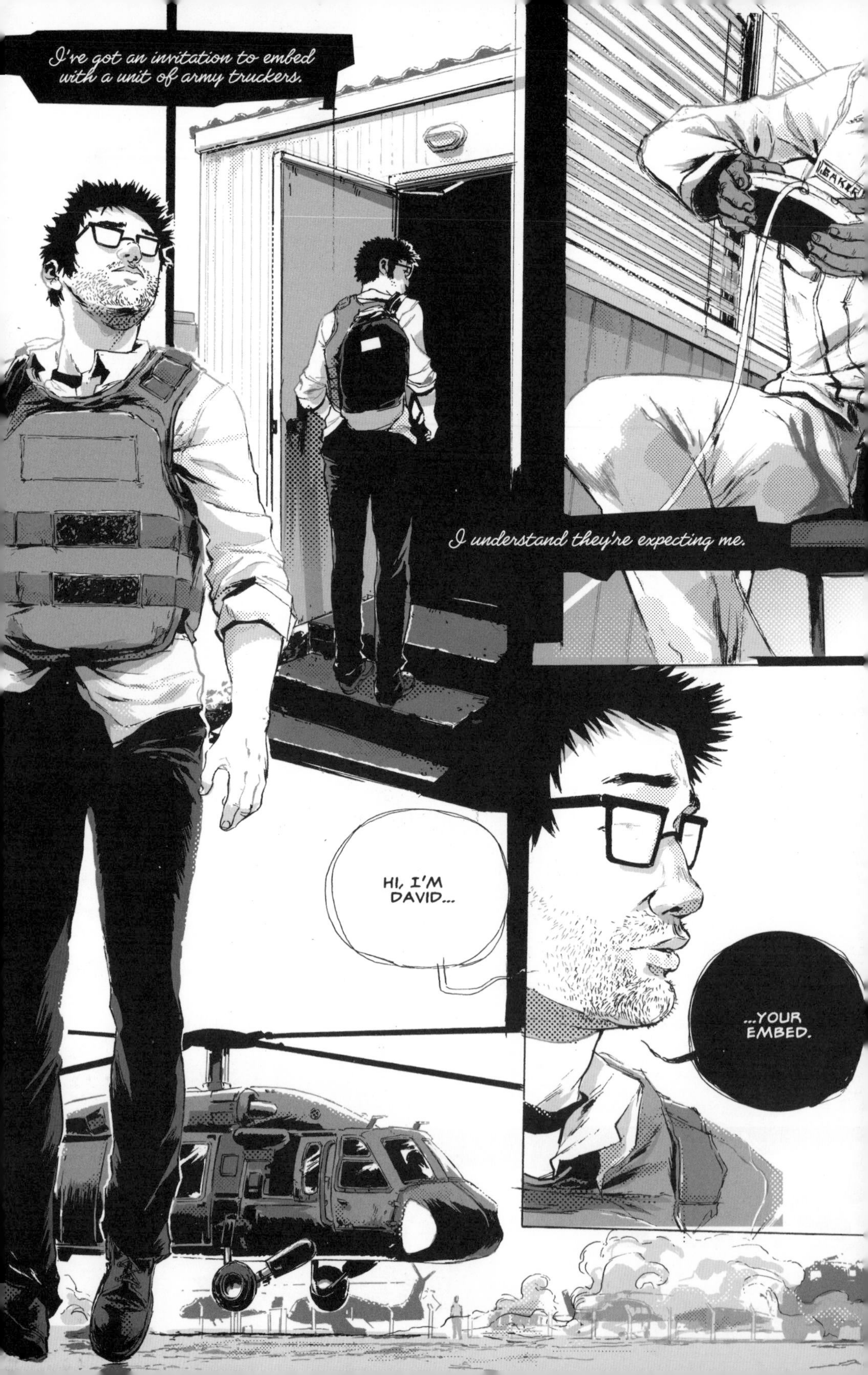
I've got an invitation to embed with a unit of army truckers.
BAKER
I understand they're expecting me.
HI, I'M DAVID...
...YOUR EMBED.

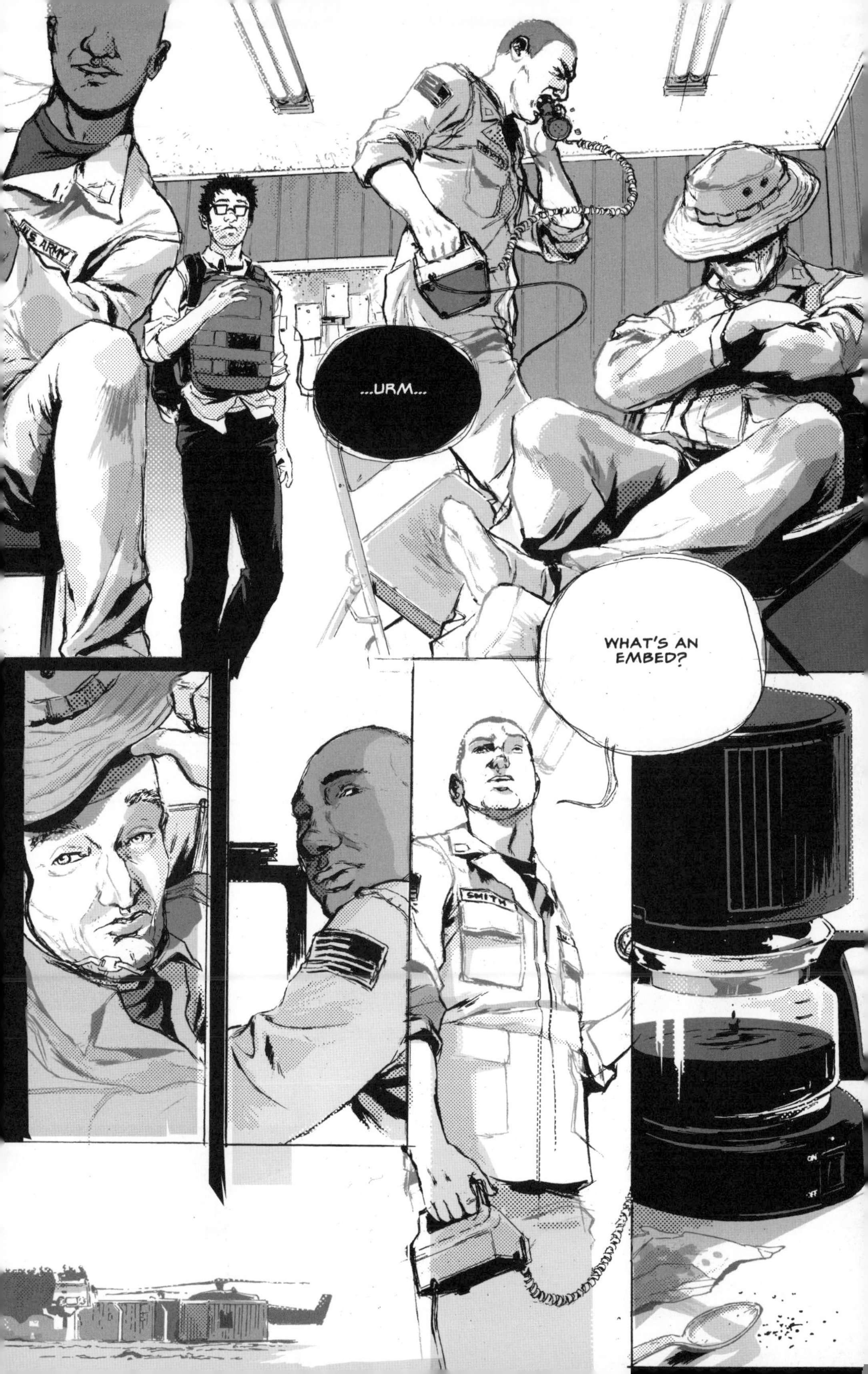
U.S. ARMY
...URM...
WHAT'S AN EMBED?
SMITH
ON
OFF

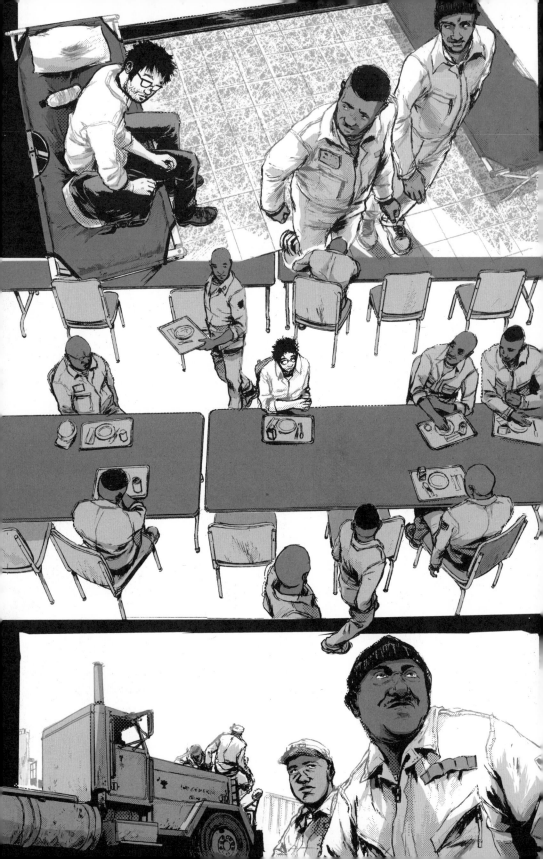

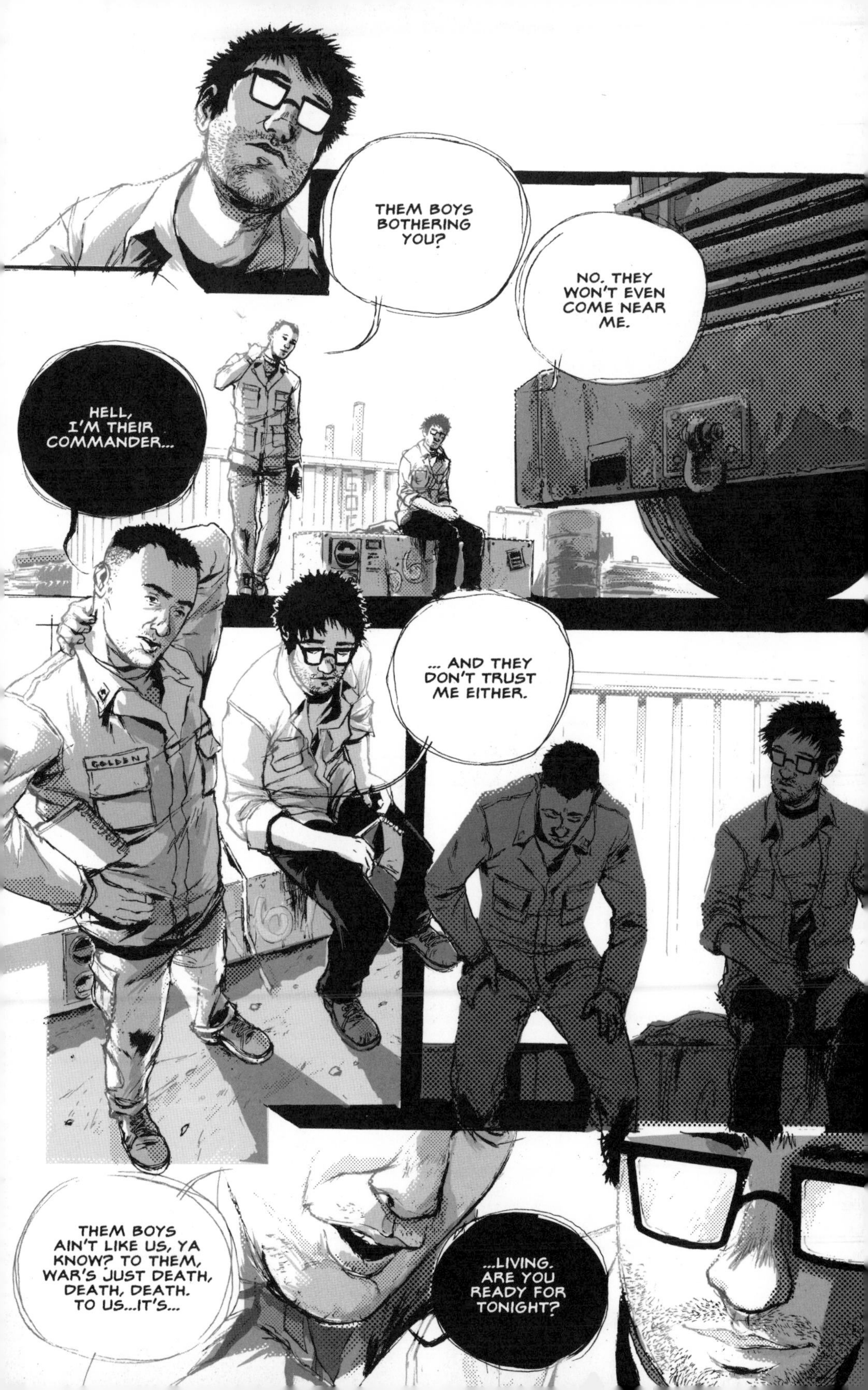
THEM BOYS BOTHERING YOU?
NO. THEY WON'T EVEN COME NEAR ME.
HELL, I'M THEIR COMMANDER...
... AND THEY DON'T TRUST ME EITHER.
THEM BOYS AIN'T LIKE US, YA KNOW? TO THEM, WAR'S JUST DEATH, DEATH, DEATH. TO US...IT'S...
...LIVING. ARE YOU READY FOR TONIGHT?

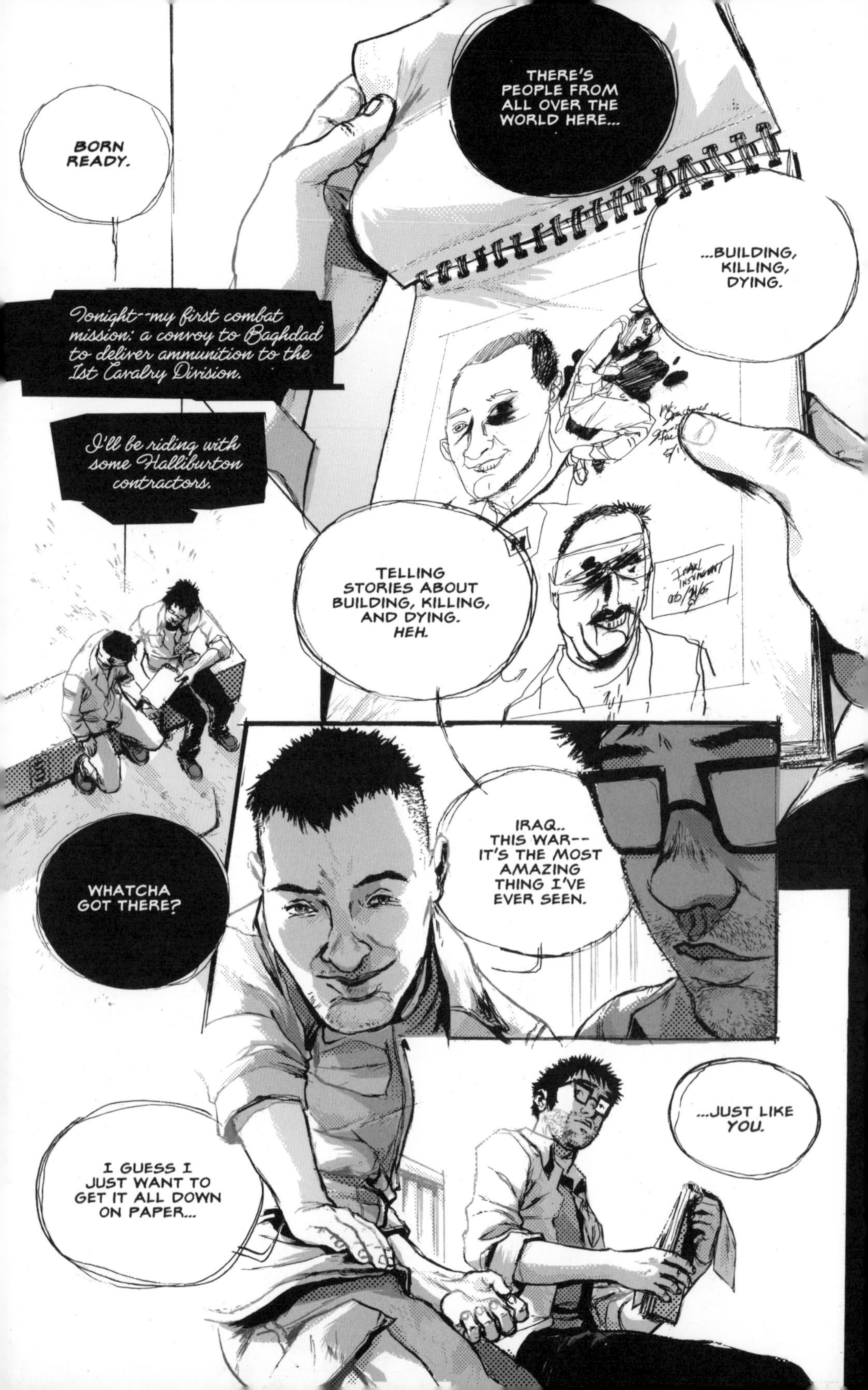
BORN READY.
THERE'S PEOPLE FROM ALL OVER THE WORLD HERE...
...BUILDING, KILLING, DYING.
Tonight--my first combat mission: a convoy to Baghdad to deliver ammunition to the 1st Cavalry Division.
I'll be riding with some Halliburton contractors.
TELLING STORIES ABOUT BUILDING, KILLING, AND DYING. HEH.
WHATCHA GOT THERE?
IRAQ.. THIS WAR-- IT'S THE MOST AMAZING THING I'VE EVER SEEN.
I GUESS I JUST WANT TO GET IT ALL DOWN ON PAPER...
...JUST LIKE YOU.

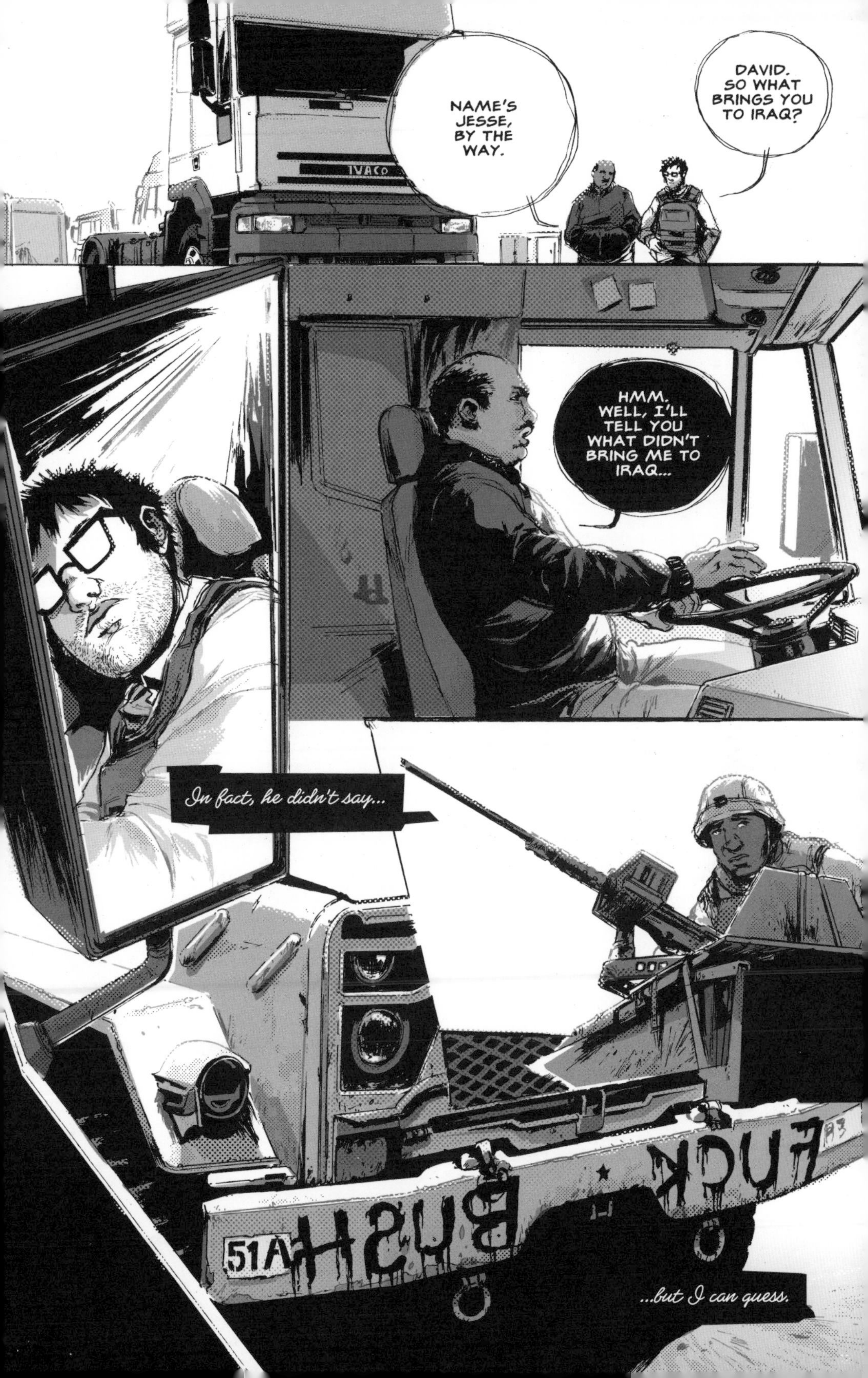
NAME'S JESSE, BY THE WAY.
DAVID. SO WHAT BRINGS YOU TO IRAQ?
HMM. WELL, I'LL TELL YOU WHAT DIDN'T BRING ME TO IRAQ...
In fact, he didn't say...
...but I can guess.

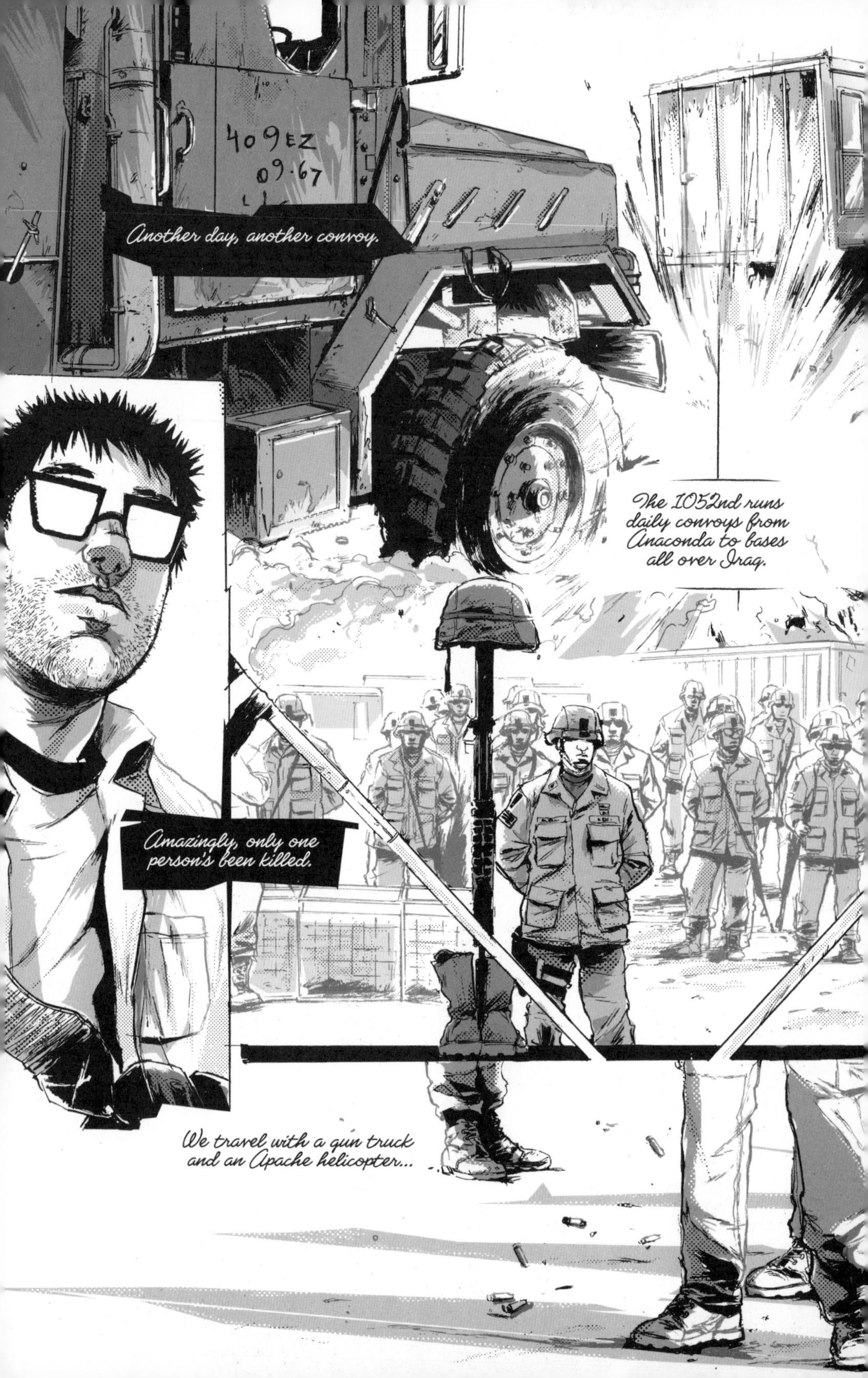
409EZ
09·67
Another day, another convoy.
The 1052nd runs daily convoys from Anaconda to bases all over Iraq.
Amazingly, only one person's been killed.
We travel with a gun truck and an Apache helicopter...

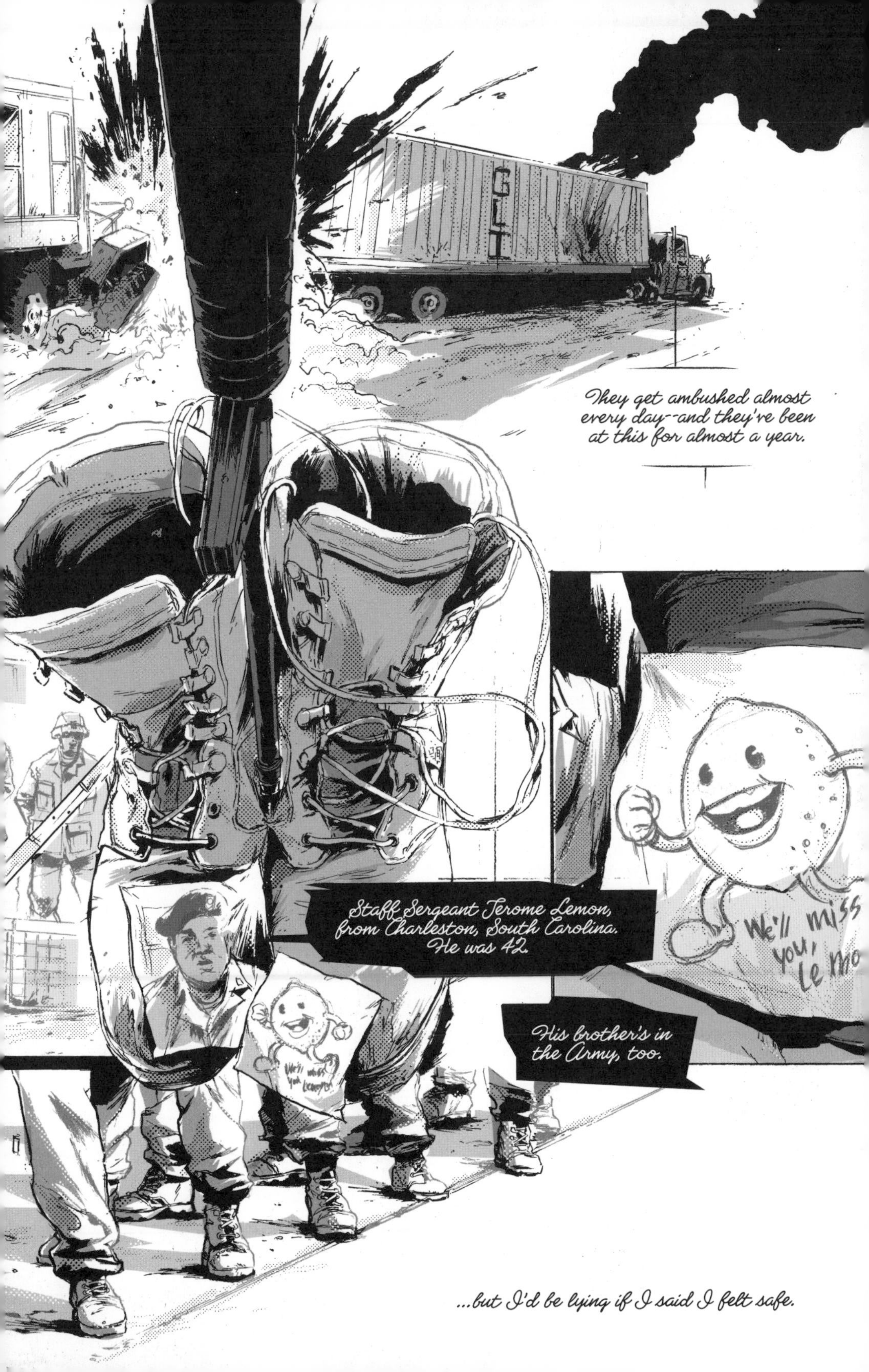

GLT
They get ambushed almost every day--and they've been at this for almost a year.
Staff Sergeant Jerome Lemon, from Charleston, South Carolina. He was 42.
We'll miss you, Lemo
His brother's in the Army, too.
...but I'd be lying if I said I felt safe.

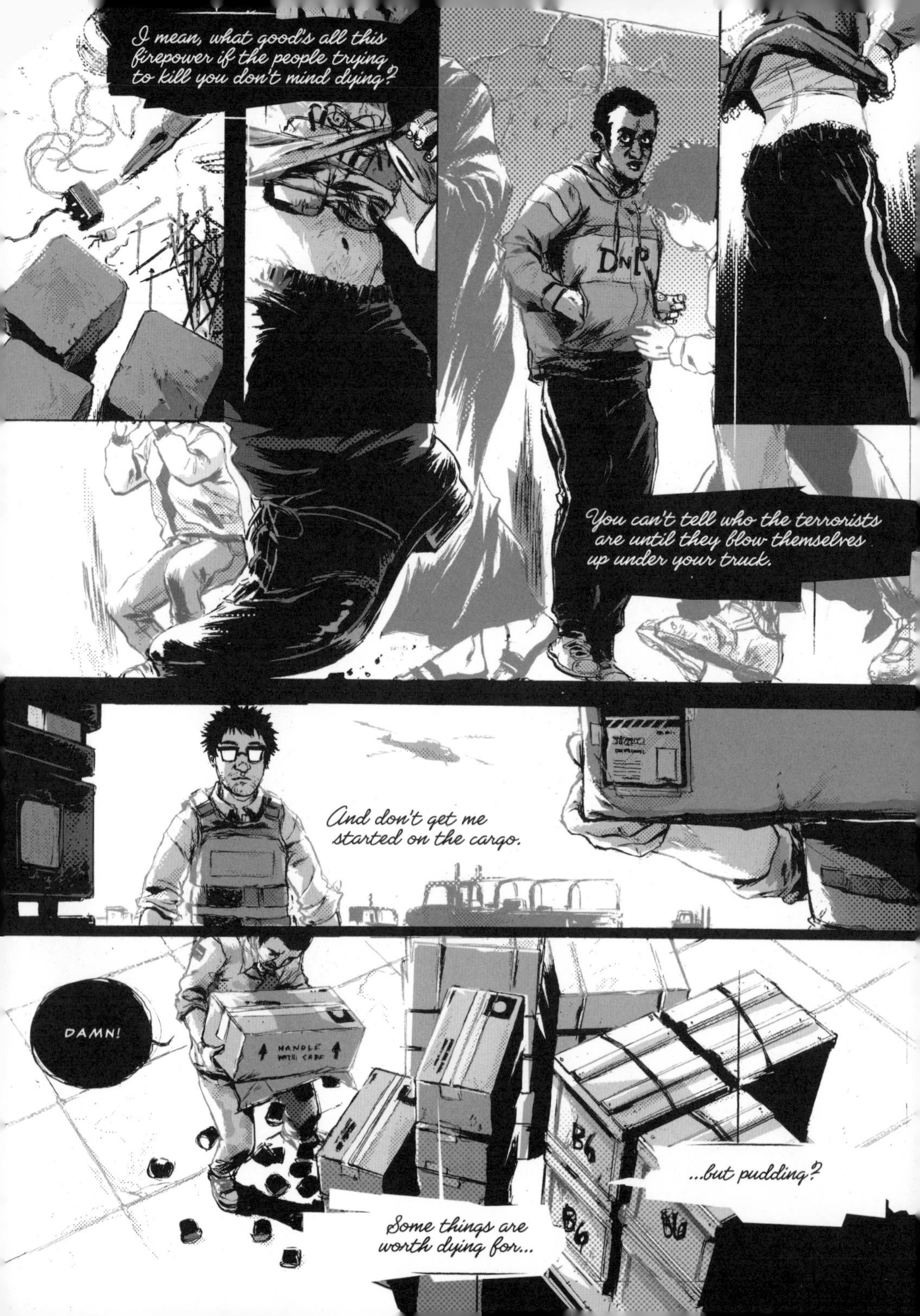
I mean, what good's all this firepower if the people trying to kill you don't mind dying?
DNP
You can't tell who the terrorists are until they blow themselves up under your truck.
And don't get me started on the cargo.
DAMN!
HANDLE WITH CARE
B6
B6
B6
Some things are worth dying for...
...but pudding?

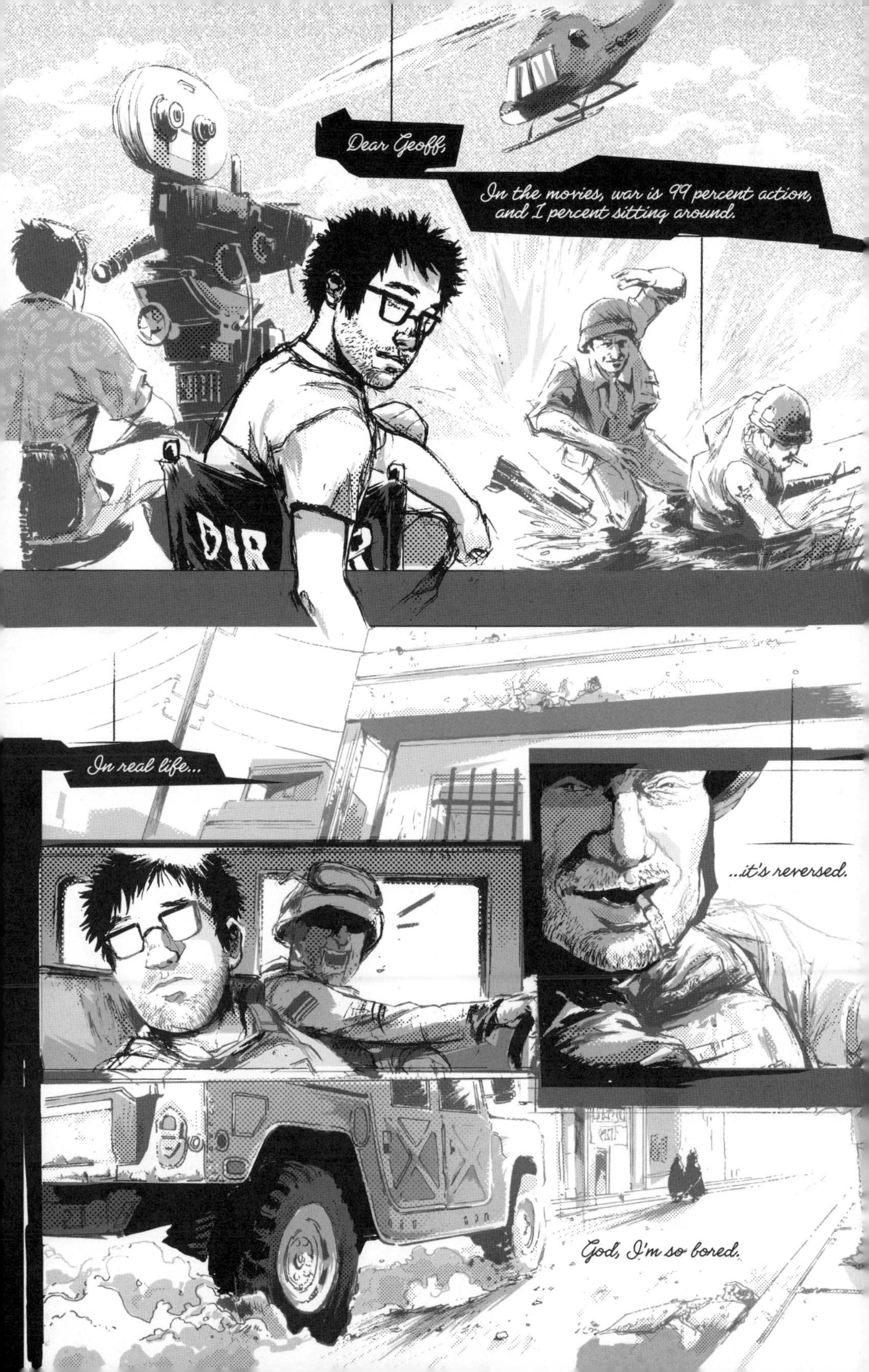

Dear Geoff,
In the movies, war is 99 percent action, and 1 percent sitting around.
DIR
In real life...
...it's reversed.
God, I'm so bored.

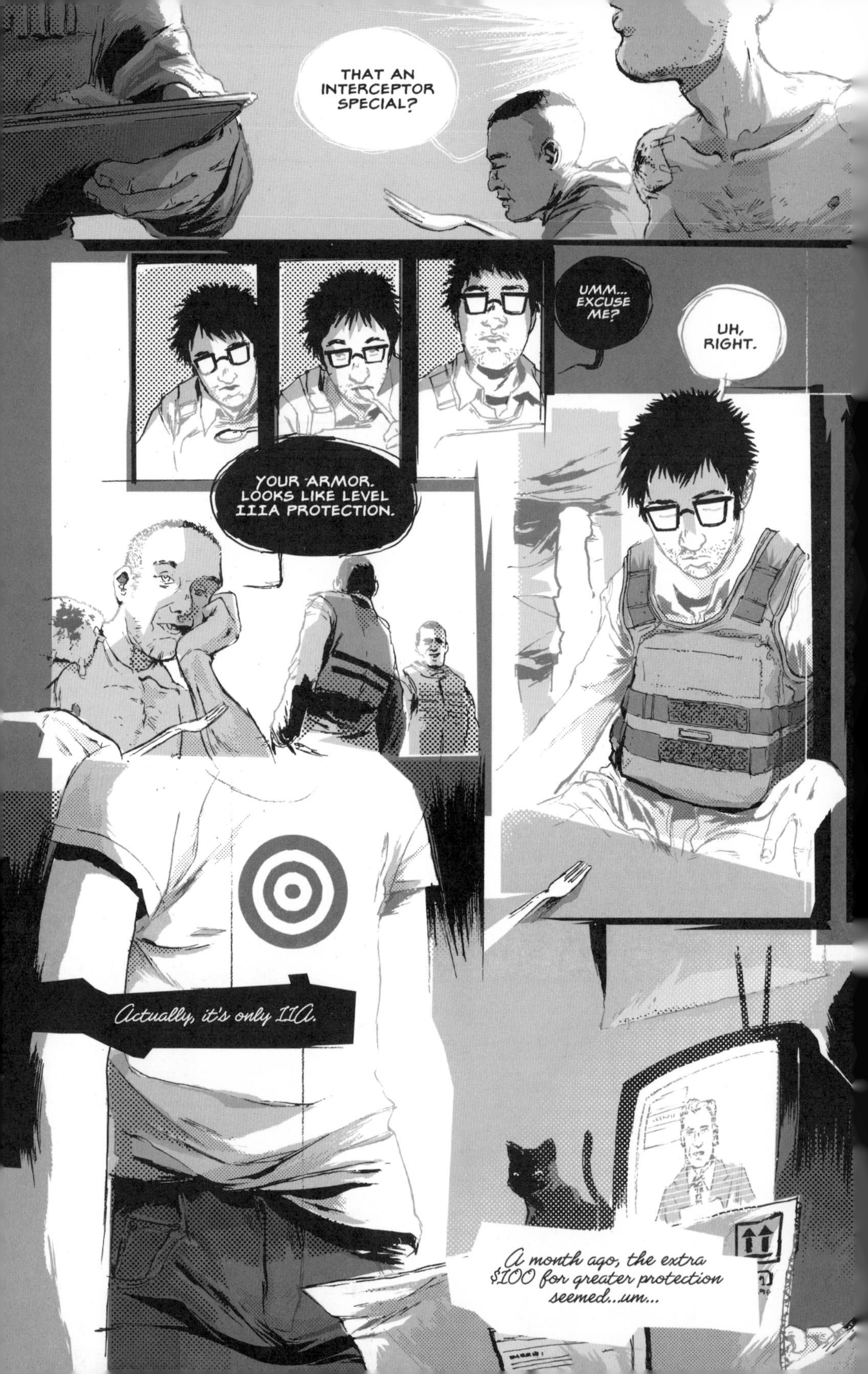
THAT AN INTERCEPTOR SPECIAL?
UMM... EXCUSE ME?
UH, RIGHT.
YOUR ARMOR. LOOKS LIKE LEVEL IIIA PROTECTION.
Actually, it's only IIA.
A month ago, the extra $100 for greater protection seemed...um...

...exorbitant.
$2000 for a roundtrip flight to Kuwait.
$100 for innoculations.
$200 for a used helmet.
$600 for a new camera.
$25 for a neato, pocketed journalist vest.
meow.

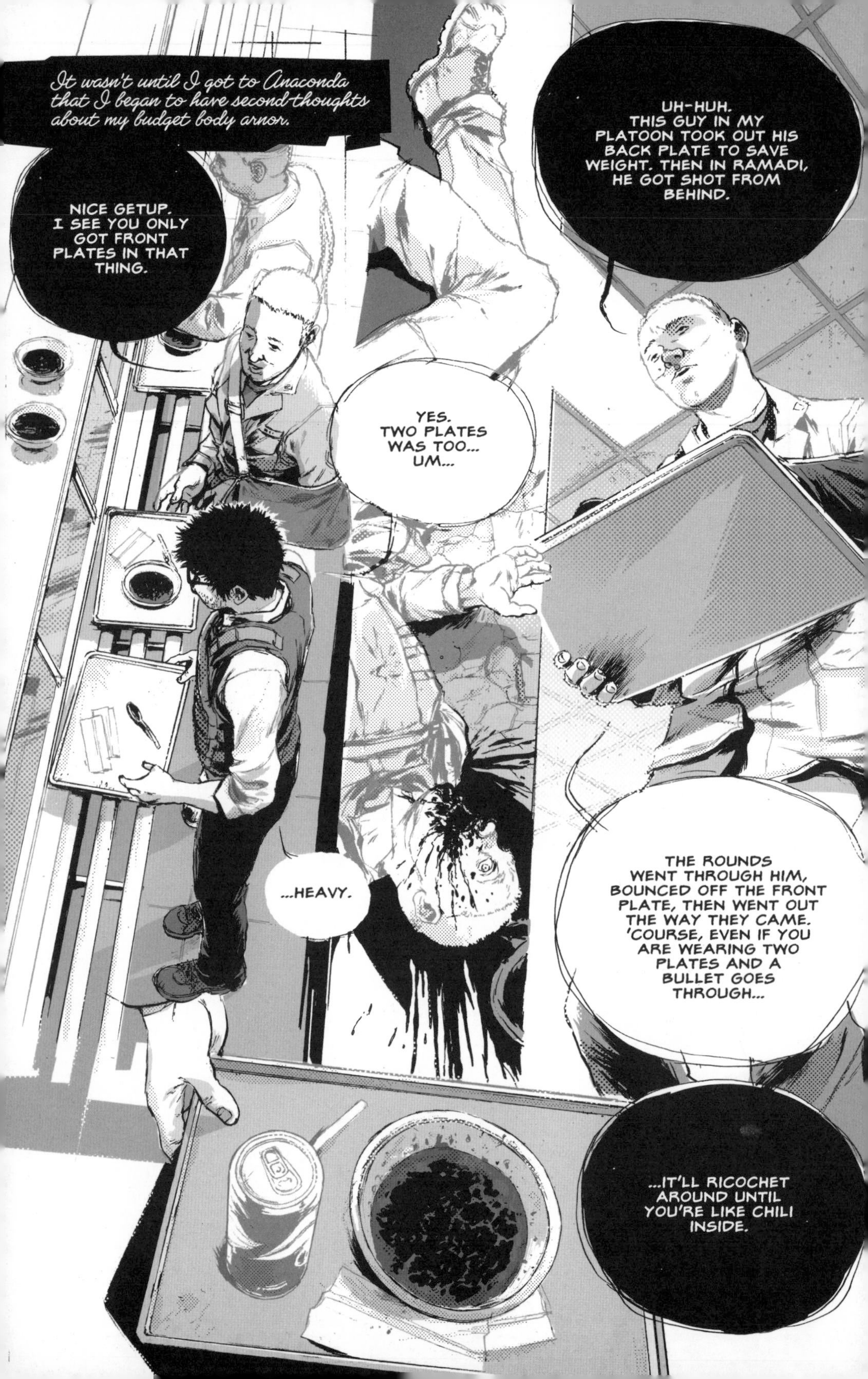
It wasn't until I got to Anaconda that I began to have second-thoughts about my budget body armor.
NICE GETUP. I SEE YOU ONLY GOT FRONT PLATES IN THAT THING.
UH-HUH. THIS GUY IN MY PLATOON TOOK OUT HIS BACK PLATE TO SAVE WEIGHT. THEN IN RAMADI, HE GOT SHOT FROM BEHIND.
YES. TWO PLATES WAS TOO... UM...
...HEAVY.
THE ROUNDS WENT THROUGH HIM, BOUNCED OFF THE FRONT PLATE, THEN WENT OUT THE WAY THEY CAME. 'COURSE, EVEN IF YOU ARE WEARING TWO PLATES AND A BULLET GOES THROUGH...
...IT'LL RICOCHET AROUND UNTIL YOU'RE LIKE CHILI INSIDE.

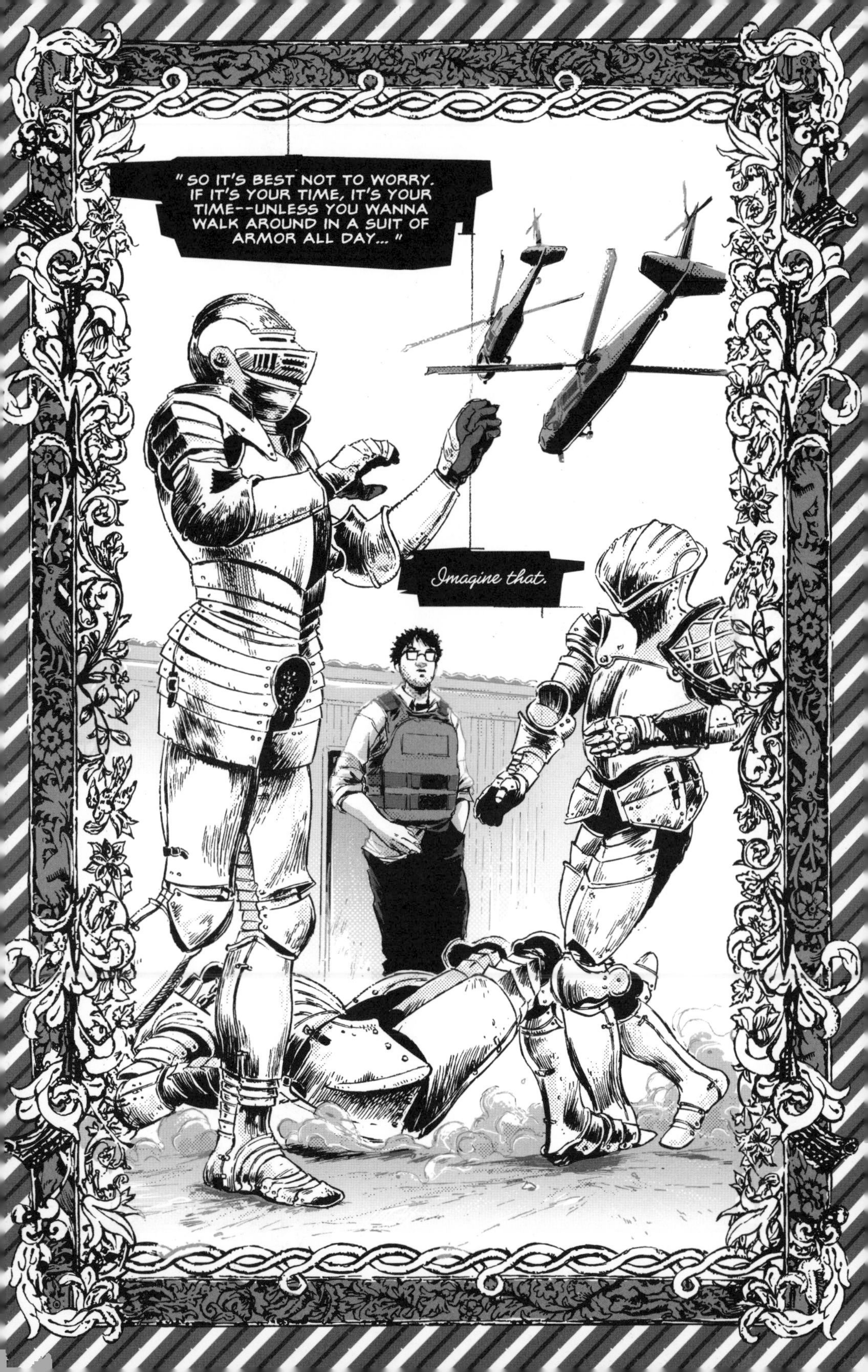
"SO IT'S BEST NOT TO WORRY. IF IT'S YOUR TIME, IT'S YOUR TIME--UNLESS YOU WANNA WALK AROUND IN A SUIT OF ARMOR ALL DAY..."
Imagine that.

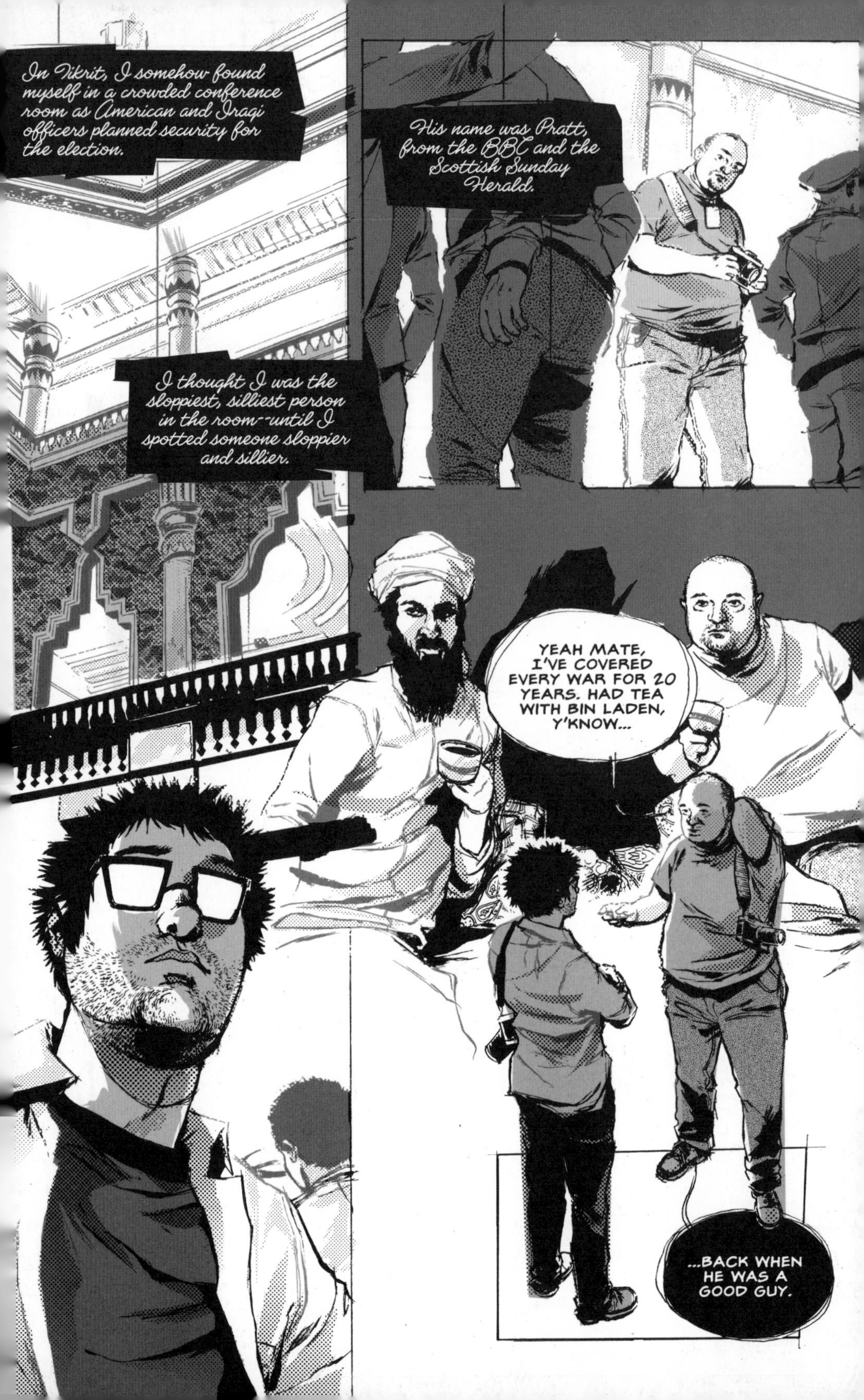
In Tikrit, I somehow found myself in a crowded conference room as American and Iraqi officers planned security for the election.
His name was Pratt, from the BBC and the Scottish Sunday Herald.
I thought I was the sloppiest, silliest person in the room--until I spotted someone sloppier and sillier.
YEAH MATE, I'VE COVERED EVERY WAR FOR 20 YEARS. HAD TEA WITH BIN LADEN, Y'KNOW...
...BACK WHEN HE WAS A GOOD GUY.

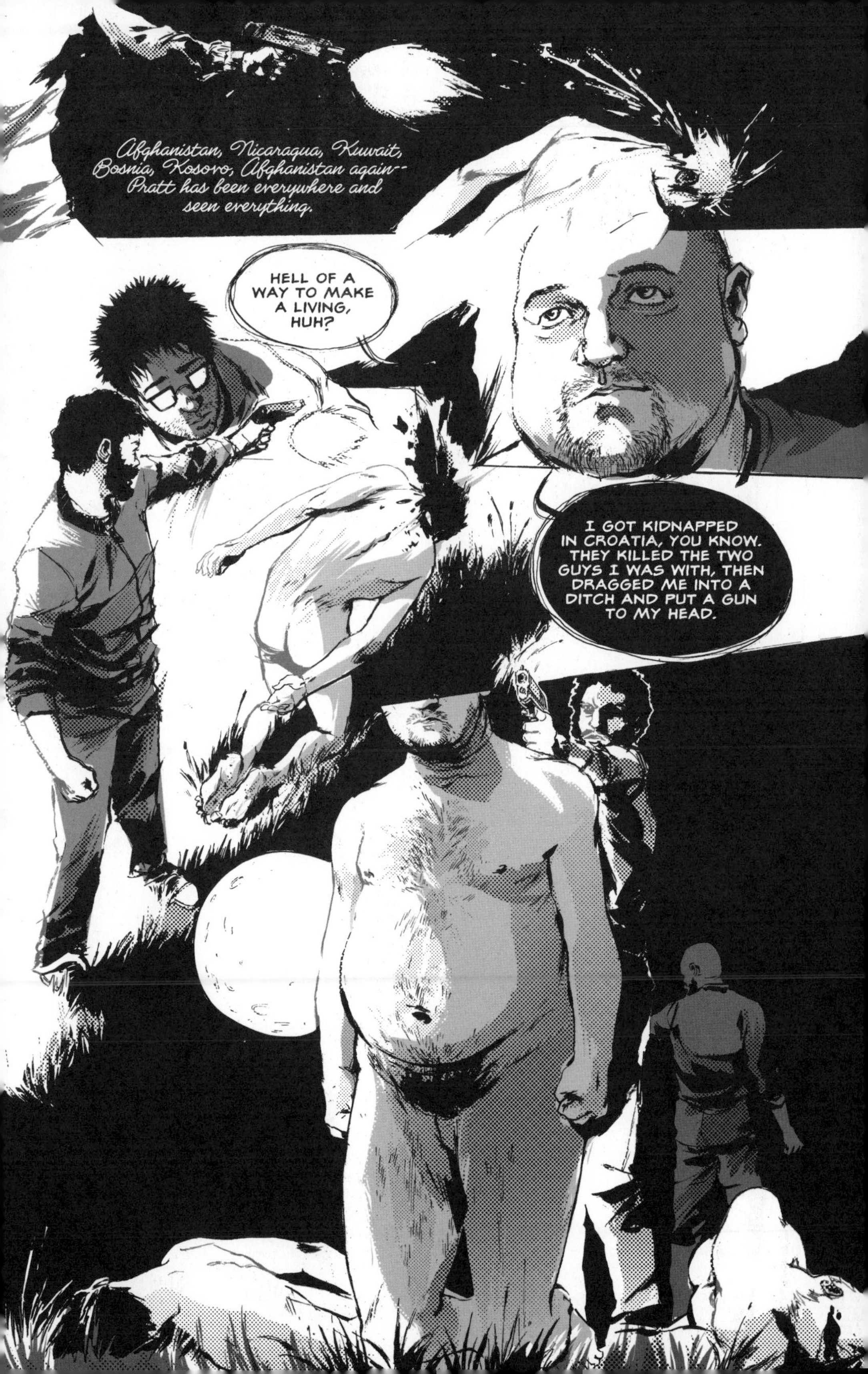
Afghanistan, Nicaragua, Kuwait, Bosnia, Kosovo, Afghanistan again--Pratt has been everywhere and seen everything.
HELL OF A WAY TO MAKE A LIVING, HUH?
I GOT KIDNAPPED IN CROATIA, YOU KNOW. THEY KILLED THE TWO GUYS I WAS WITH, THEN DRAGGED ME INTO A DITCH AND PUT A GUN TO MY HEAD.

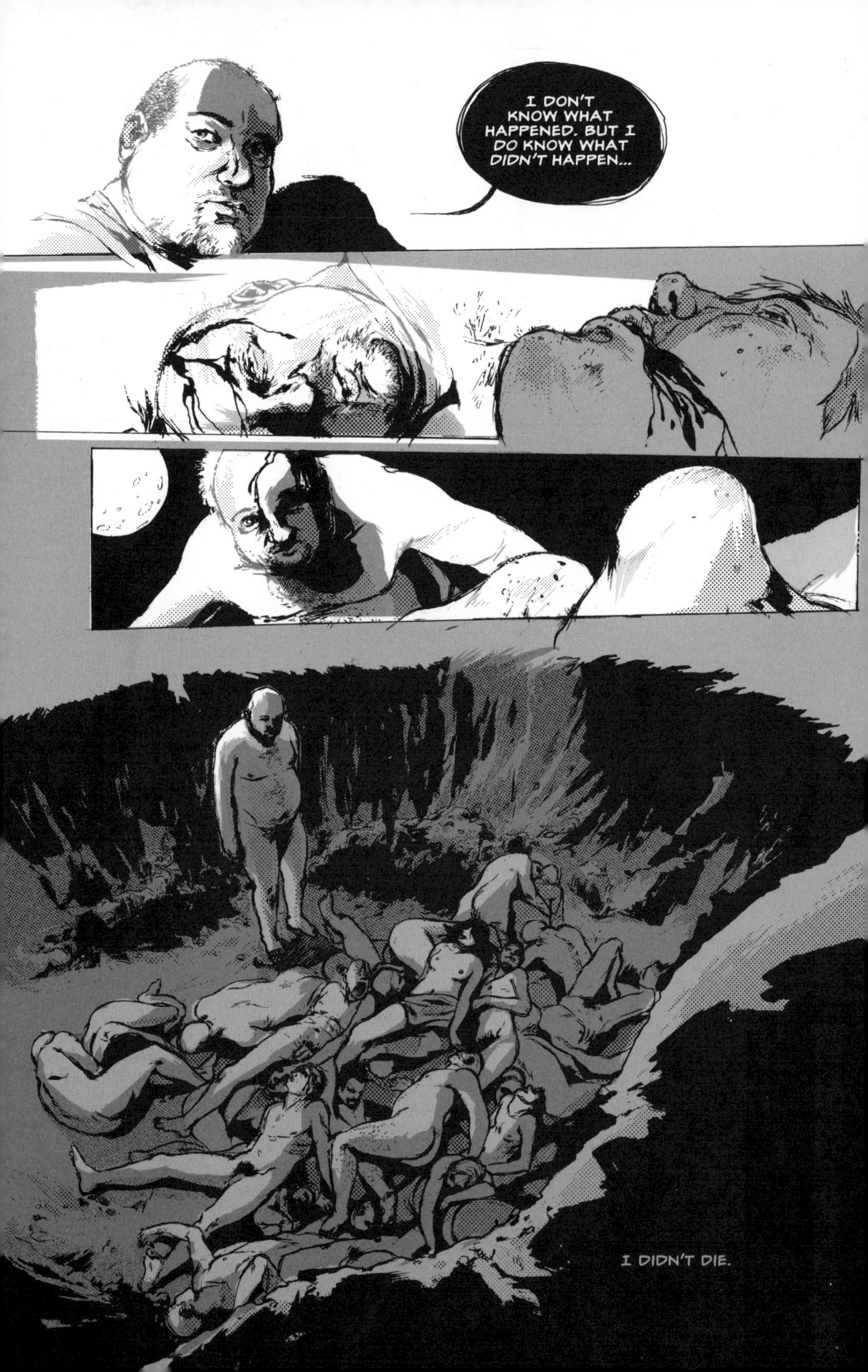
I DON'T KNOW WHAT HAPPENED. BUT I DO KNOW WHAT DIDN'T HAPPEN...
I DIDN'T DIE.

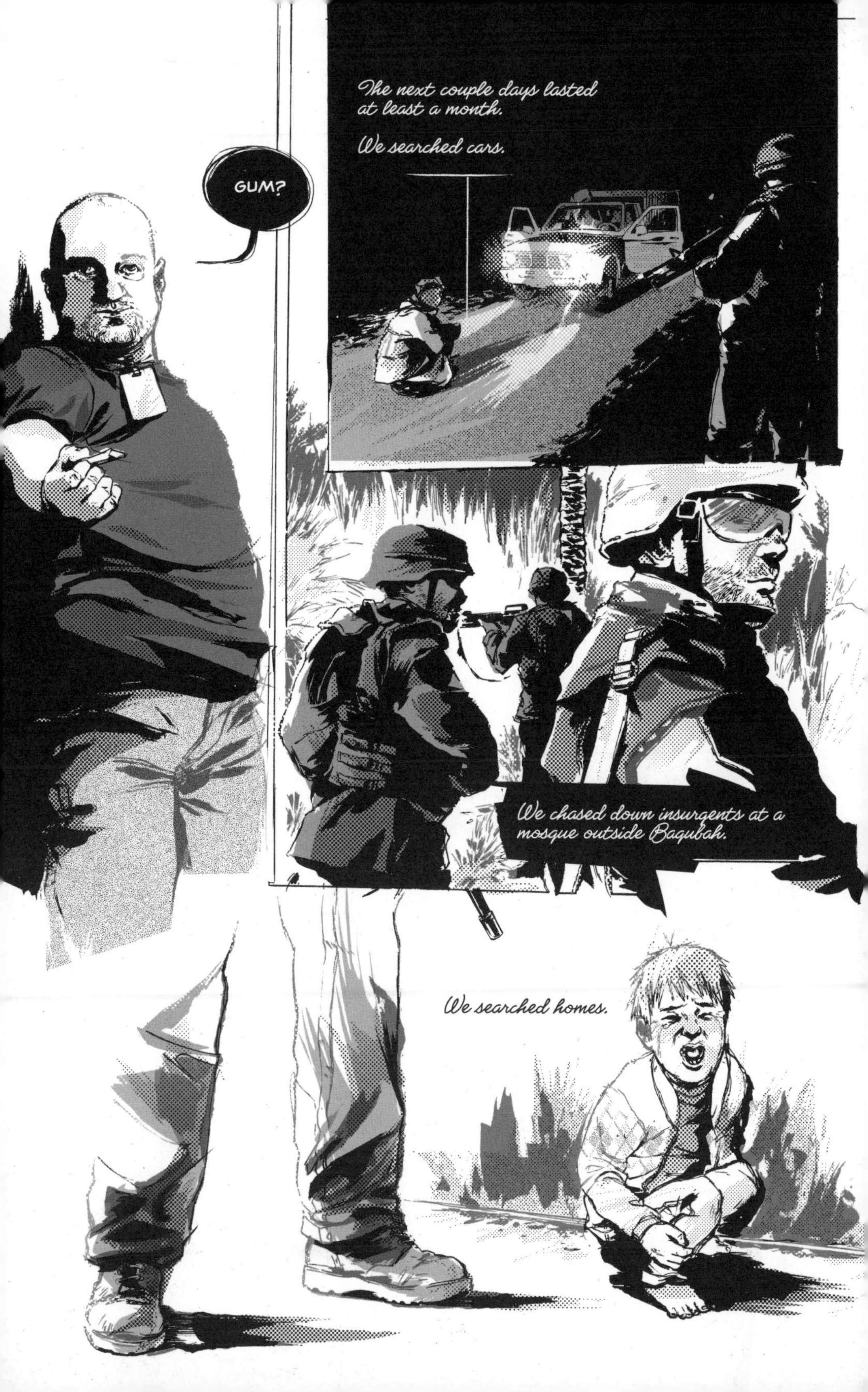
The next couple days lasted at least a month.
We searched cars.
GUM?
We chased down insurgents at a mosque outside Baqubah.
We searched homes.

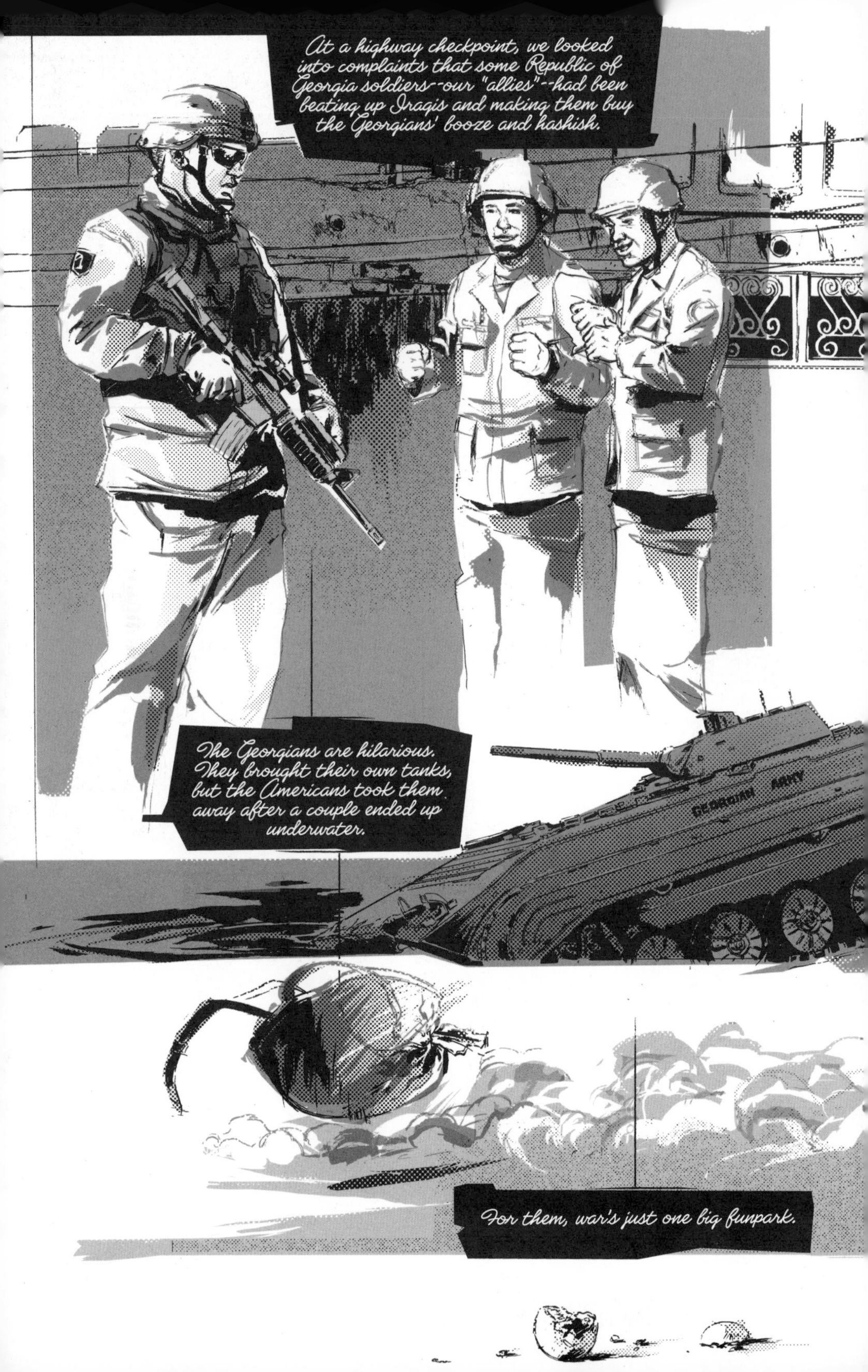
At a highway checkpoint, we looked into complaints that some Republic of Georgia soldiers--our "allies"--had been beating up Iraqis and making them buy the Georgians' booze and hashish.
The Georgians are hilarious. They brought their own tanks, but the Americans took them away after a couple ended up underwater.
GEORGIAN ARMY
For them, war's just one big funpark.

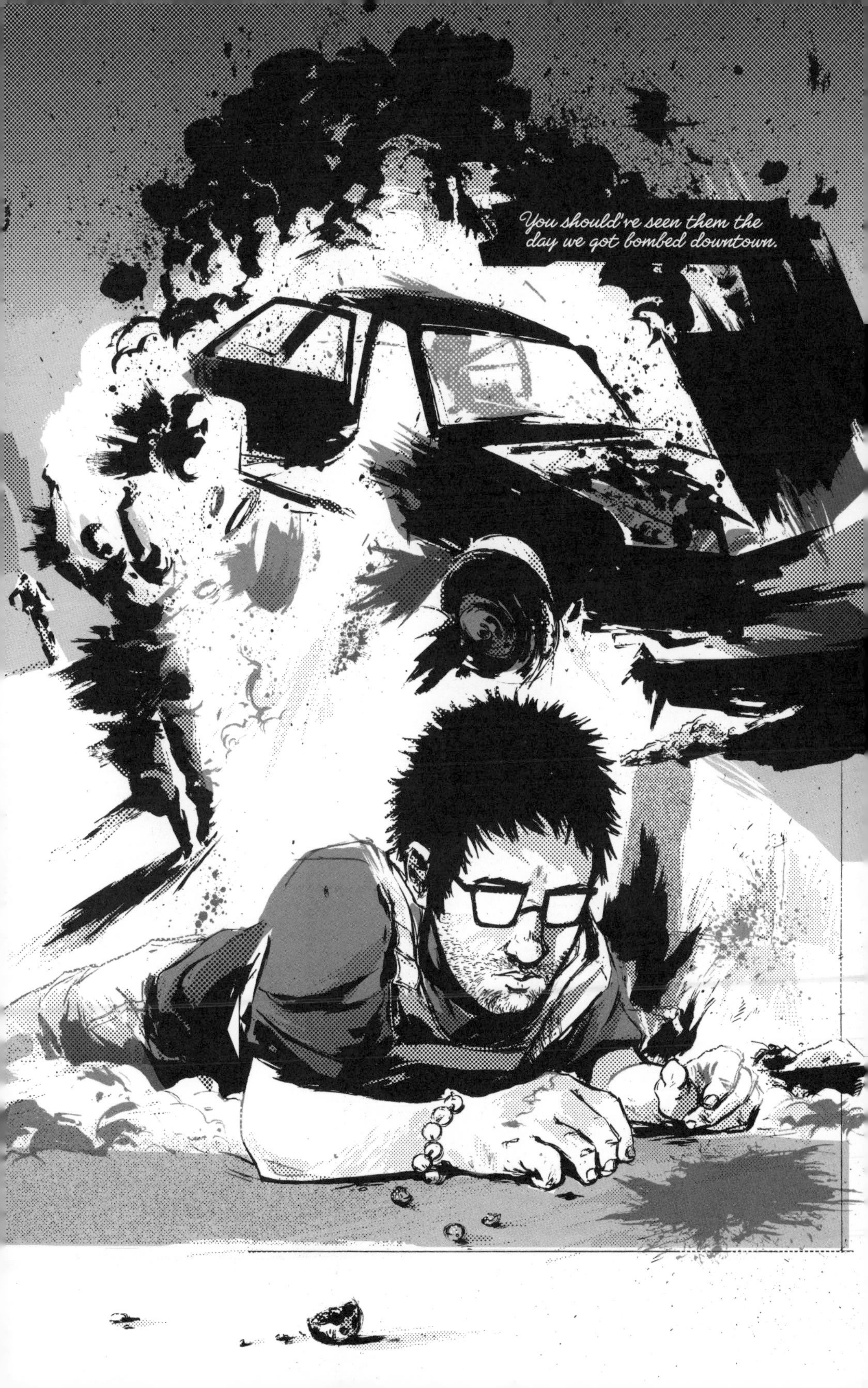
You should've seen them the day we got bombed downtown.

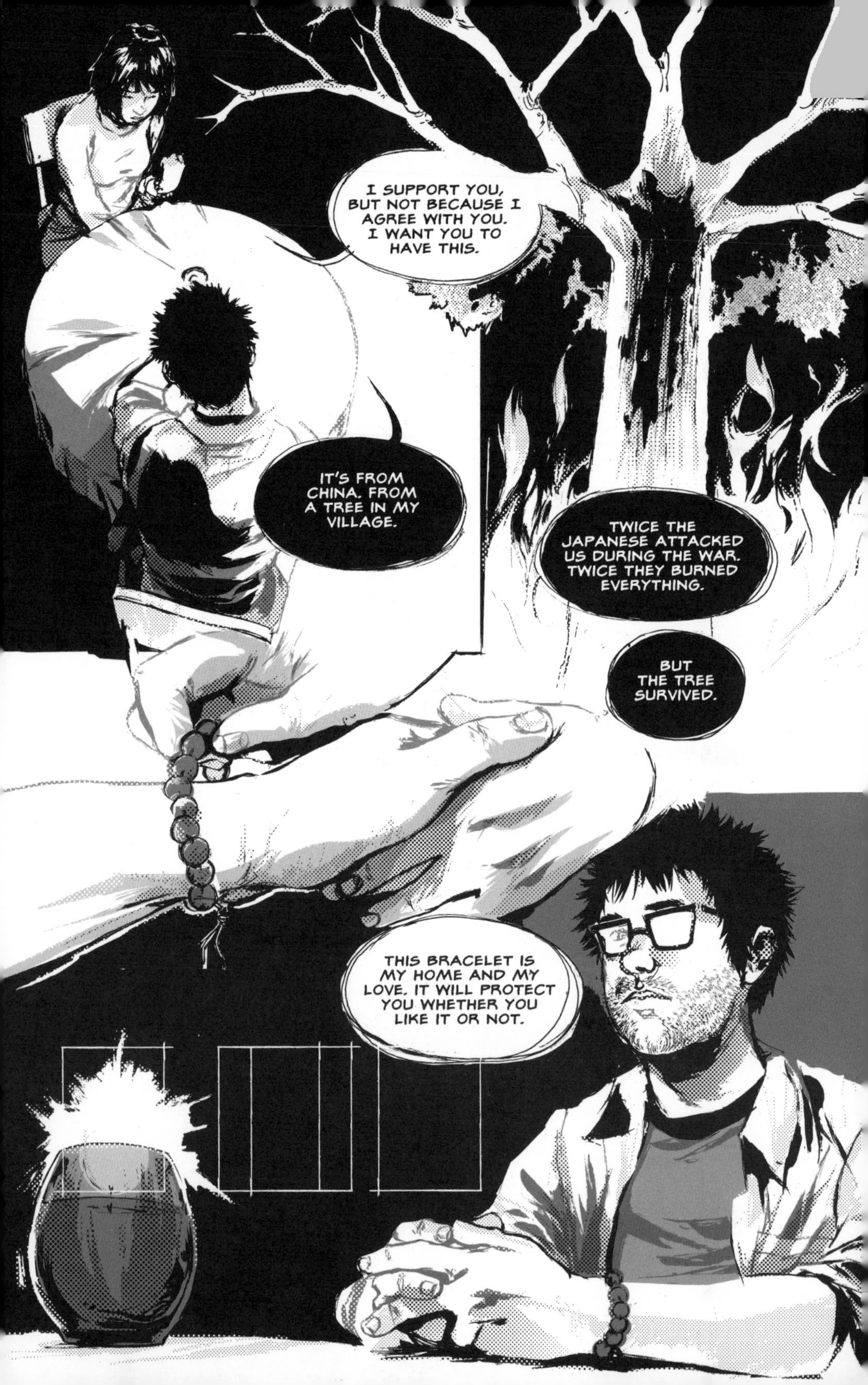
I SUPPORT YOU, BUT NOT BECAUSE I AGREE WITH YOU. I WANT YOU TO HAVE THIS.
IT'S FROM CHINA. FROM A TREE IN MY VILLAGE.
TWICE THE JAPANESE ATTACKED US DURING THE WAR. TWICE THEY BURNED EVERYTHING.
BUT THE TREE SURVIVED.
THIS BRACELET IS MY HOME AND MY LOVE. IT WILL PROTECT YOU WHETHER YOU LIKE IT OR NOT.

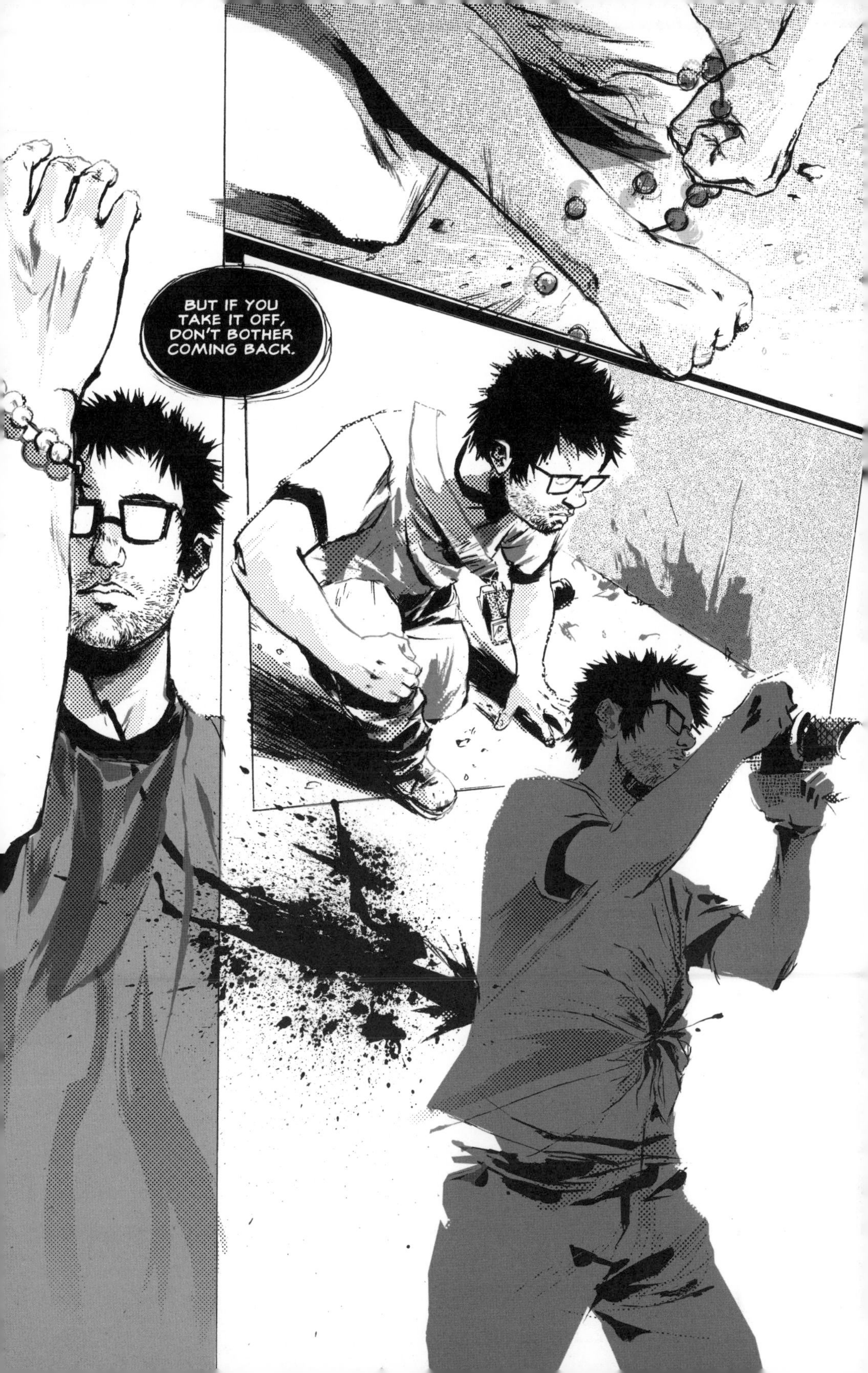
BUT IF YOU TAKE IT OFF, DON'T BOTHER COMING BACK.

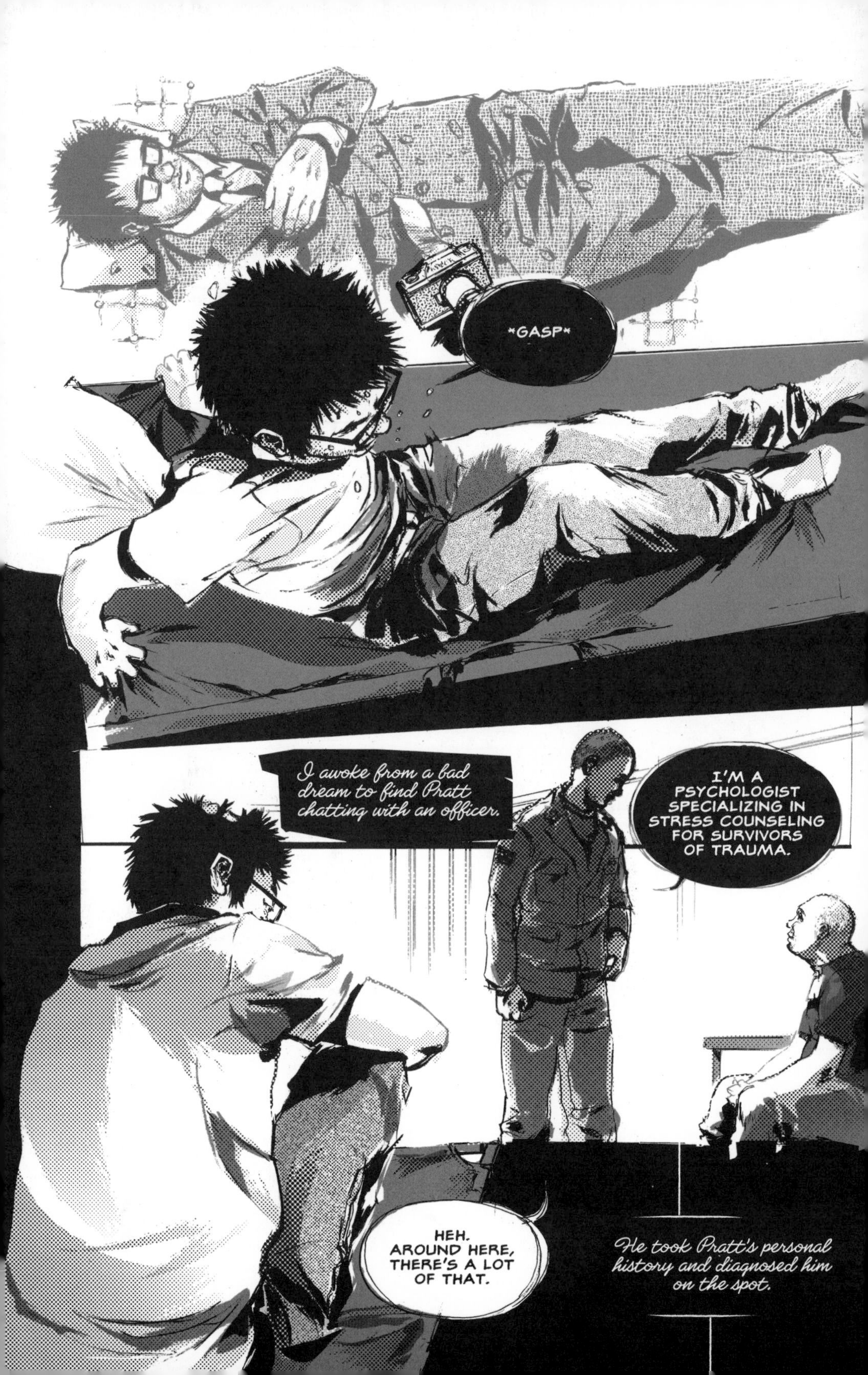
GASP
I awoke from a bad dream to find Pratt chatting with an officer.
I'M A PSYCHOLOGIST SPECIALIZING IN STRESS COUNSELING FOR SURVIVORS OF TRAUMA.
HEH. AROUND HERE, THERE'S A LOT OF THAT.
He took Pratt's personal history and diagnosed him on the spot.

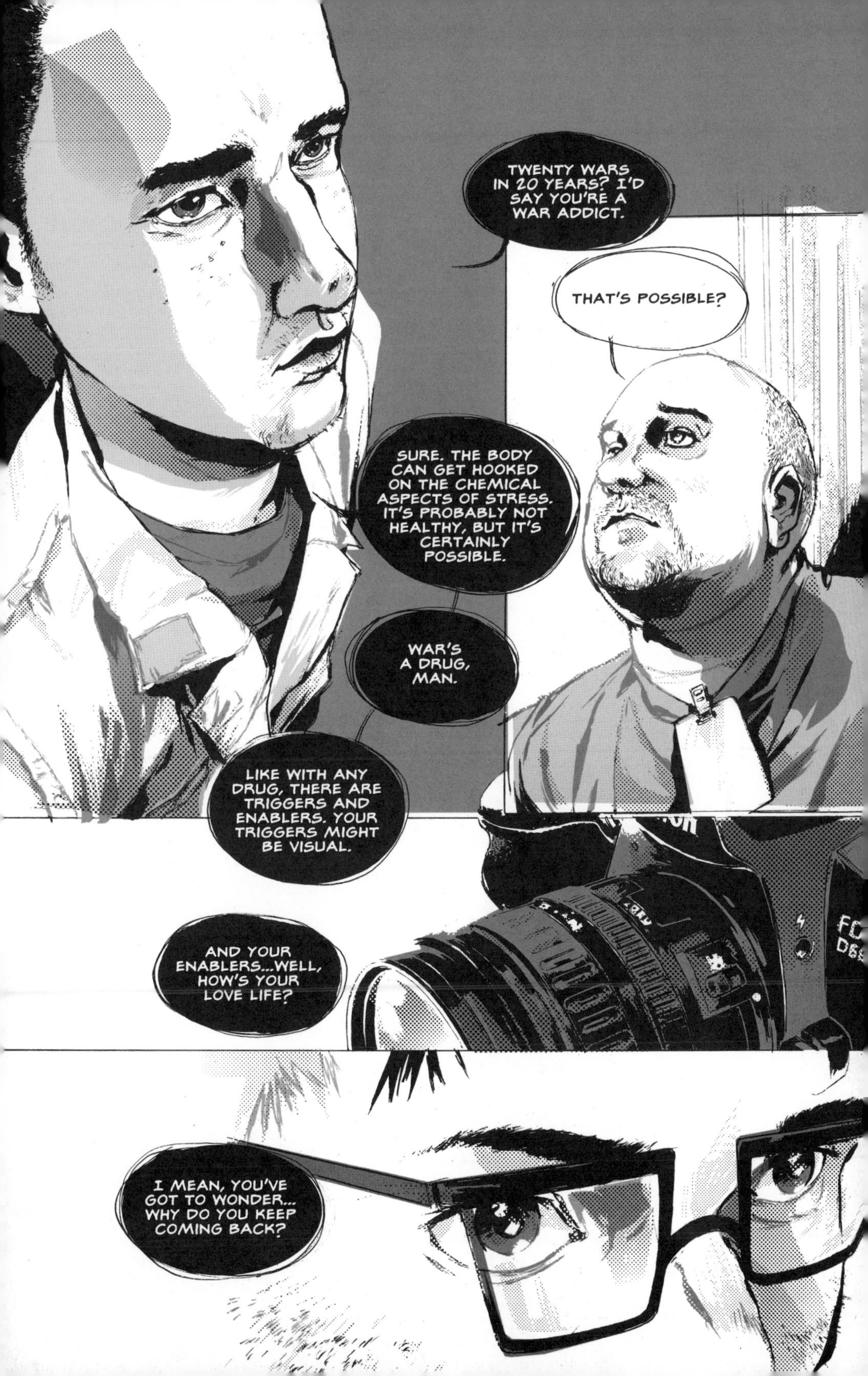
TWENTY WARS IN 20 YEARS? I'D SAY YOU'RE A WAR ADDICT.
THAT'S POSSIBLE?
SURE. THE BODY CAN GET HOOKED ON THE CHEMICAL ASPECTS OF STRESS. IT'S PROBABLY NOT HEALTHY, BUT IT'S CERTAINLY POSSIBLE.
WAR'S A DRUG, MAN.
LIKE WITH ANY DRUG, THERE ARE TRIGGERS AND ENABLERS. YOUR TRIGGERS MIGHT BE VISUAL.
AND YOUR ENABLERS...WELL, HOW'S YOUR LOVE LIFE?
I MEAN, YOU'VE GOT TO WONDER... WHY DO YOU KEEP COMING BACK?

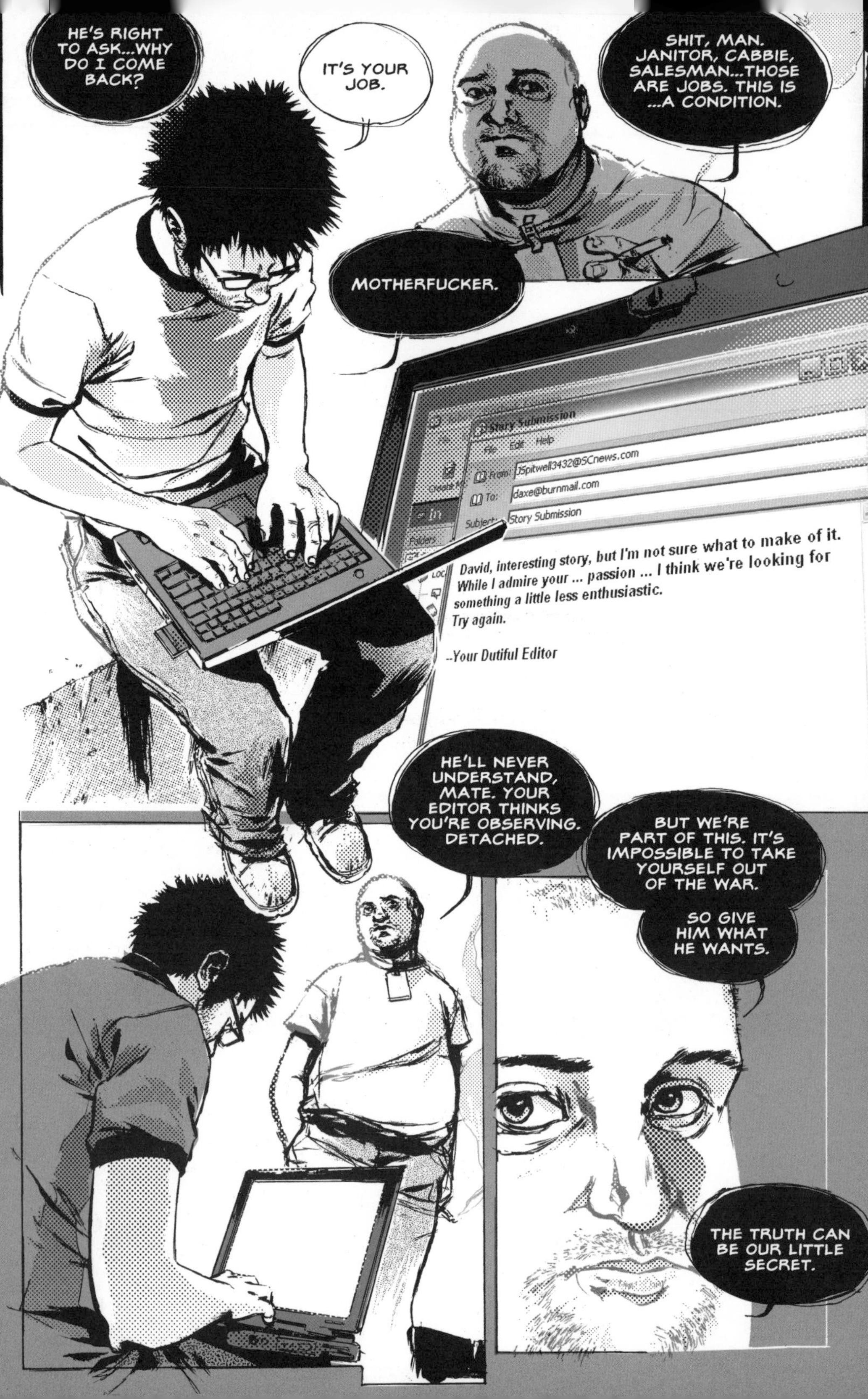

HE'S RIGHT TO ASK...WHY DO I COME BACK?
IT'S YOUR JOB.
SHIT, MAN. JANITOR, CABBIE, SALESMAN...THOSE ARE JOBS. THIS IS ...A CONDITION.
MOTHERFUCKER.
Story Submission
File Edit Help
From: JSpitwell3432@SCnews.com
To: daxe@burnmail.com
Subject: Story Submission
David, interesting story, but I'm not sure what to make of it. While I admire your ... passion ... I think we're looking for something a little less enthusiastic.
Try again.
--Your Dutiful Editor
HE'LL NEVER UNDERSTAND, MATE. YOUR EDITOR THINKS YOU'RE OBSERVING. DETACHED.
BUT WE'RE PART OF THIS. IT'S IMPOSSIBLE TO TAKE YOURSELF OUT OF THE WAR.
SO GIVE HIM WHAT HE WANTS.
THE TRUTH CAN BE OUR LITTLE SECRET.

THE M-2 BRADLEY, DUDE. GREATEST FIGHTING MACHINE IN THE WORLD.
EATS INSURGENTS FOR BREAKFAST AND CRAPS 'EM OUT THE BACK.
What he didn't say is that just a week ago, a Bradley rolled into a canal, trapping five men inside.
I JUMPED IN THE WATER TO SAVE THEM, BUT THE MUD WAS TOO DEEP.
IT WAS SO COLD...I COULD HEAR THEM SCREAMING...
OH JESUS.

They found a note on one of the bodies.
GOT MY NOTICE, MATE. I'M HEADED TO BAGHDAD.
DAVID? WHAT IS IT?
...
IT'S WONDERFUL.
THIS IS MY LIFE, I GIVE IT.

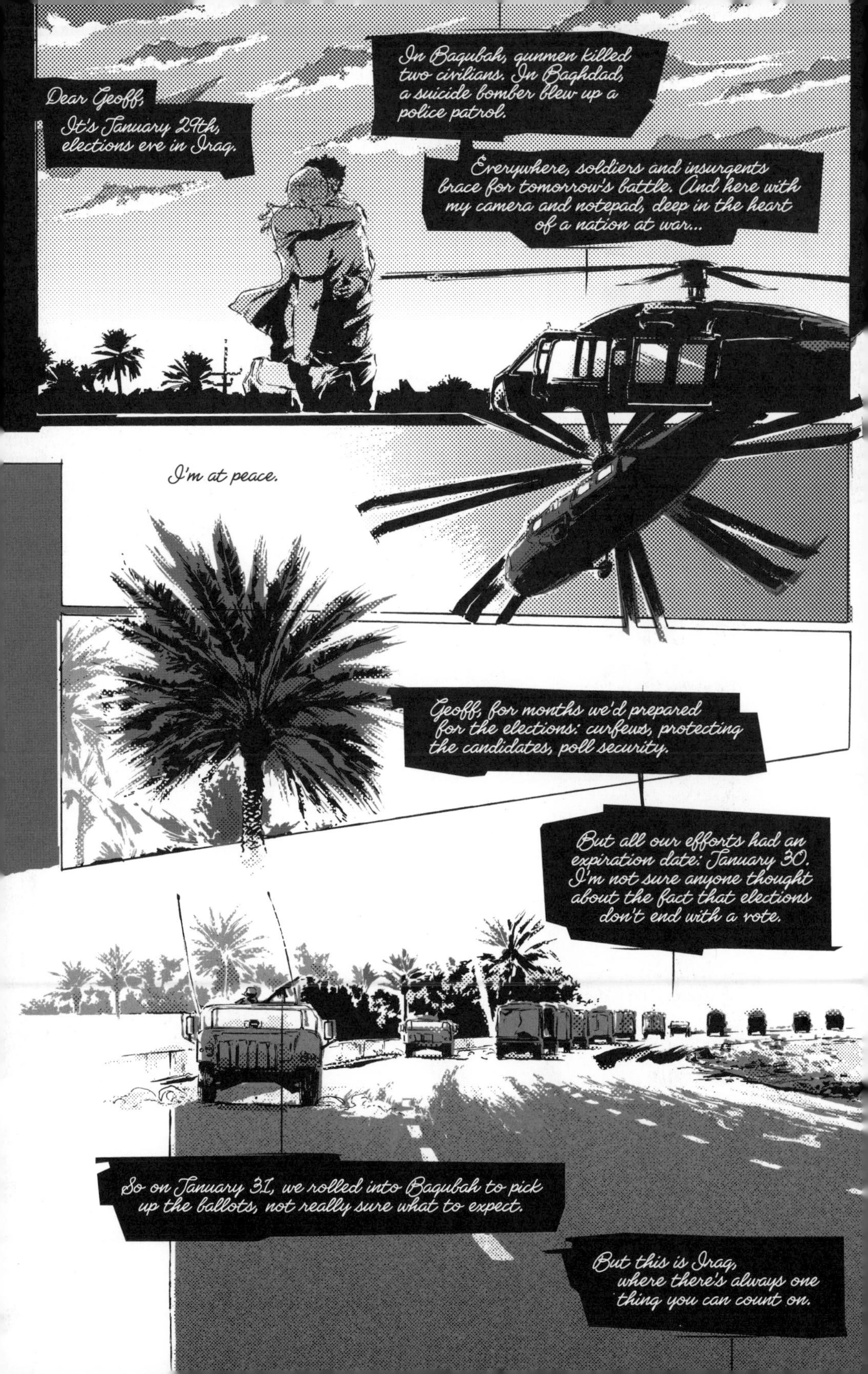
Dear Geoff,
It's January 29th, elections eve in Iraq.
In Baqubah, gunmen killed two civilians. In Baghdad, a suicide bomber blew up a police patrol.
Everywhere, soldiers and insurgents brace for tomorrow's battle. And here with my camera and notepad, deep in the heart of a nation at war...
I'm at peace.
Geoff, for months we'd prepared for the elections: curfews, protecting the candidates, poll security.
But all our efforts had an expiration date: January 30. I'm not sure anyone thought about the fact that elections don't end with a vote.
So on January 31, we rolled into Baqubah to pick up the ballots, not really sure what to expect.
But this is Iraq, where there's always one thing you can count on.

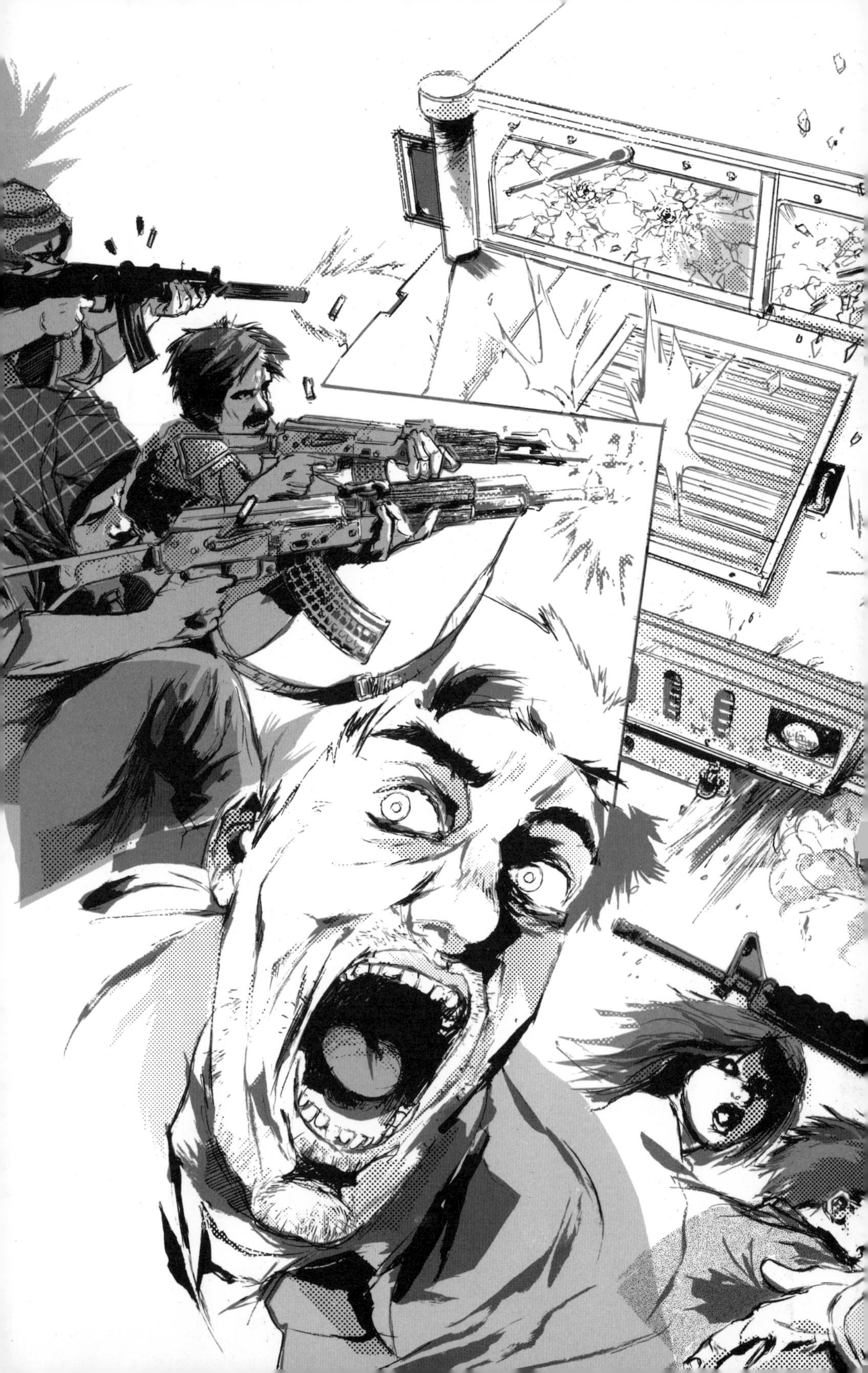

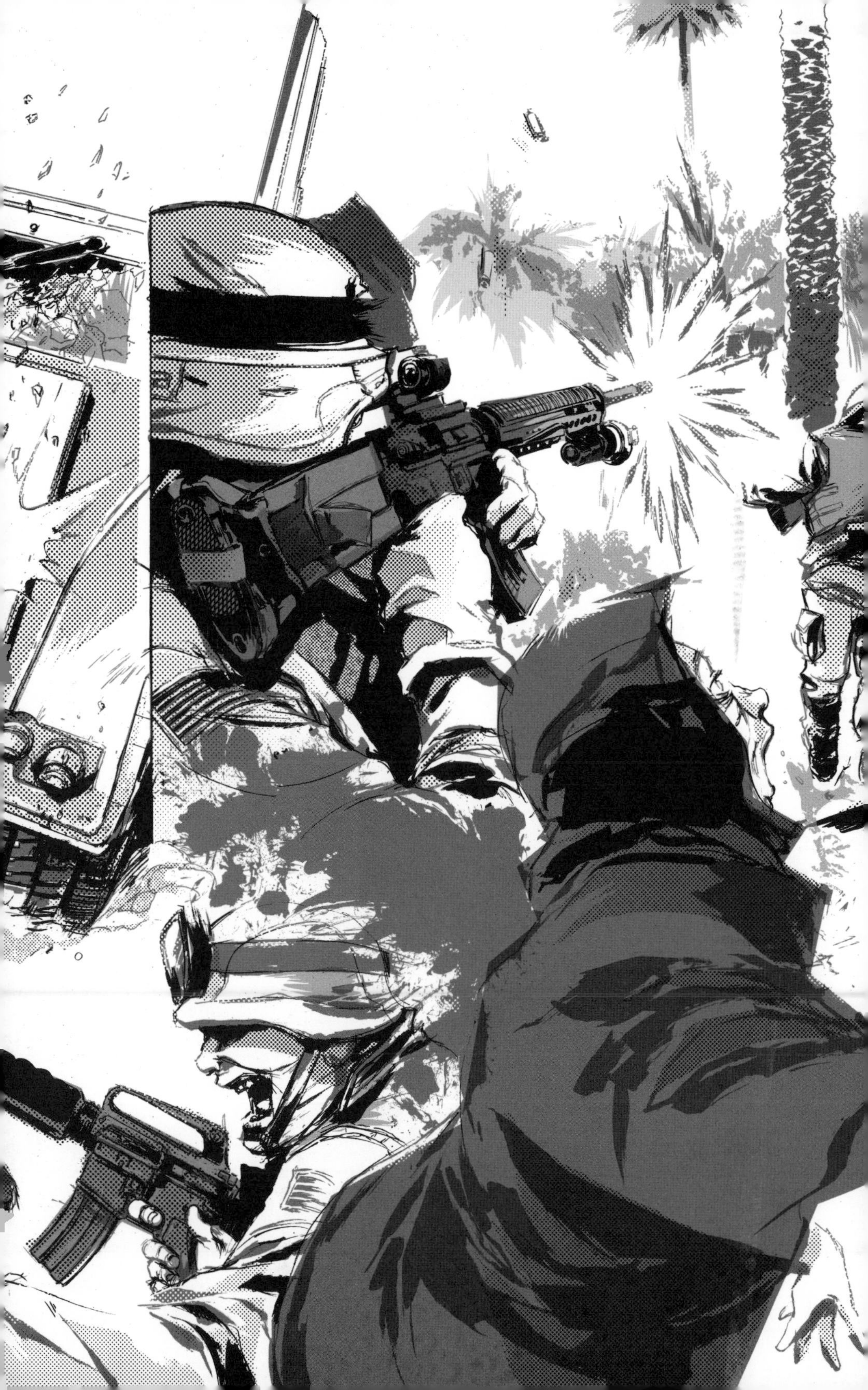

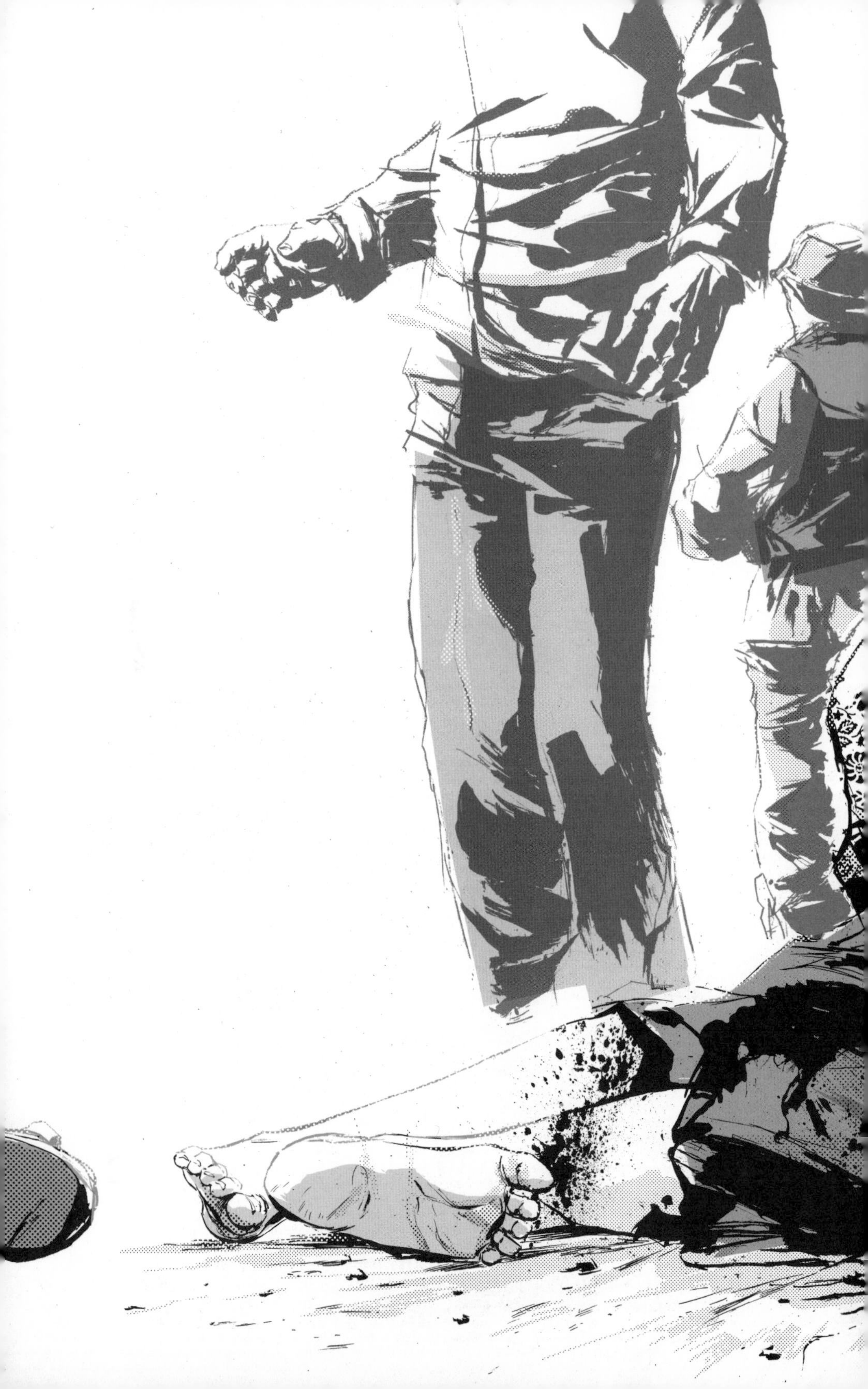

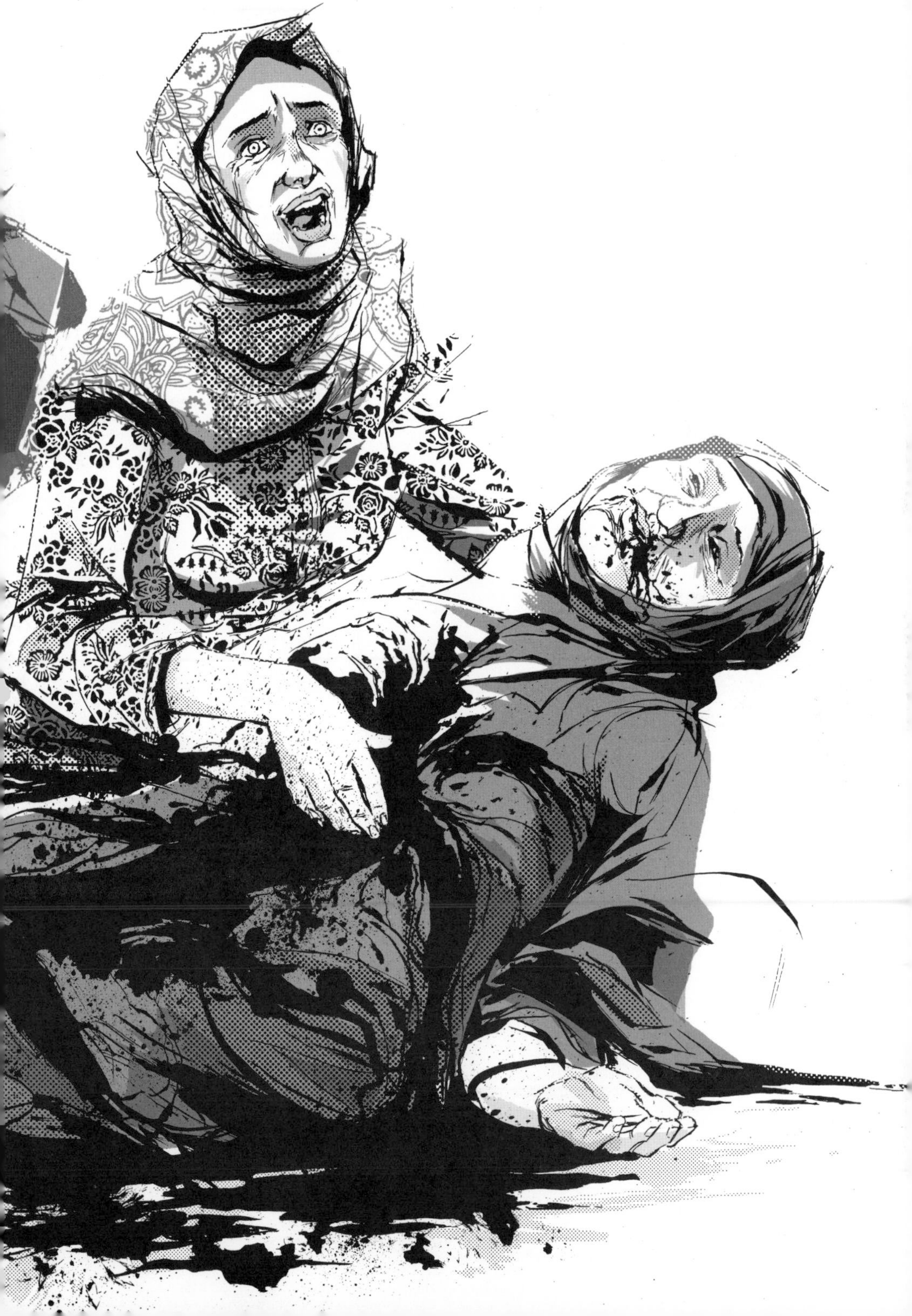

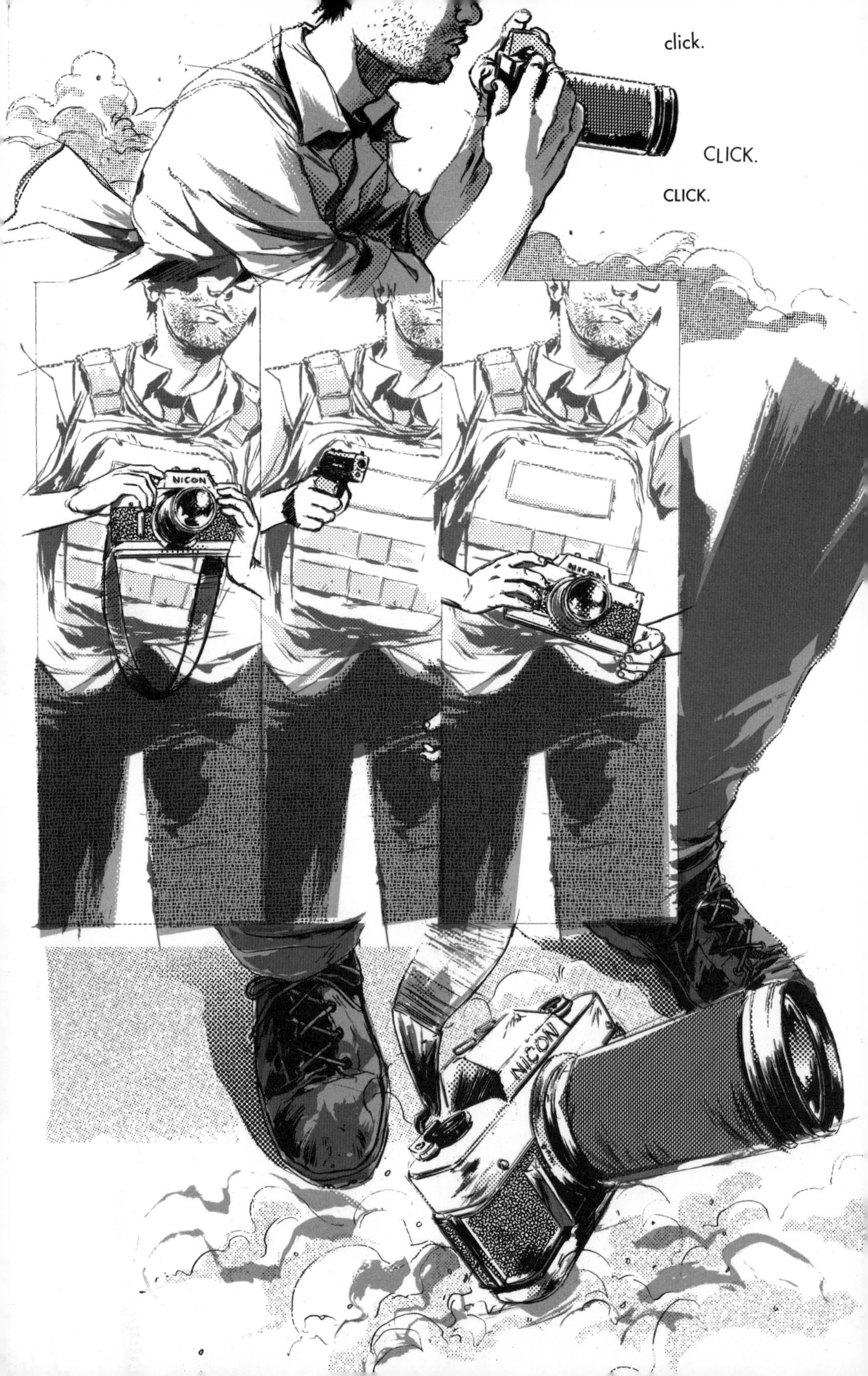
click.
CLICK.
CLICK.
NICON
NICON
NICON

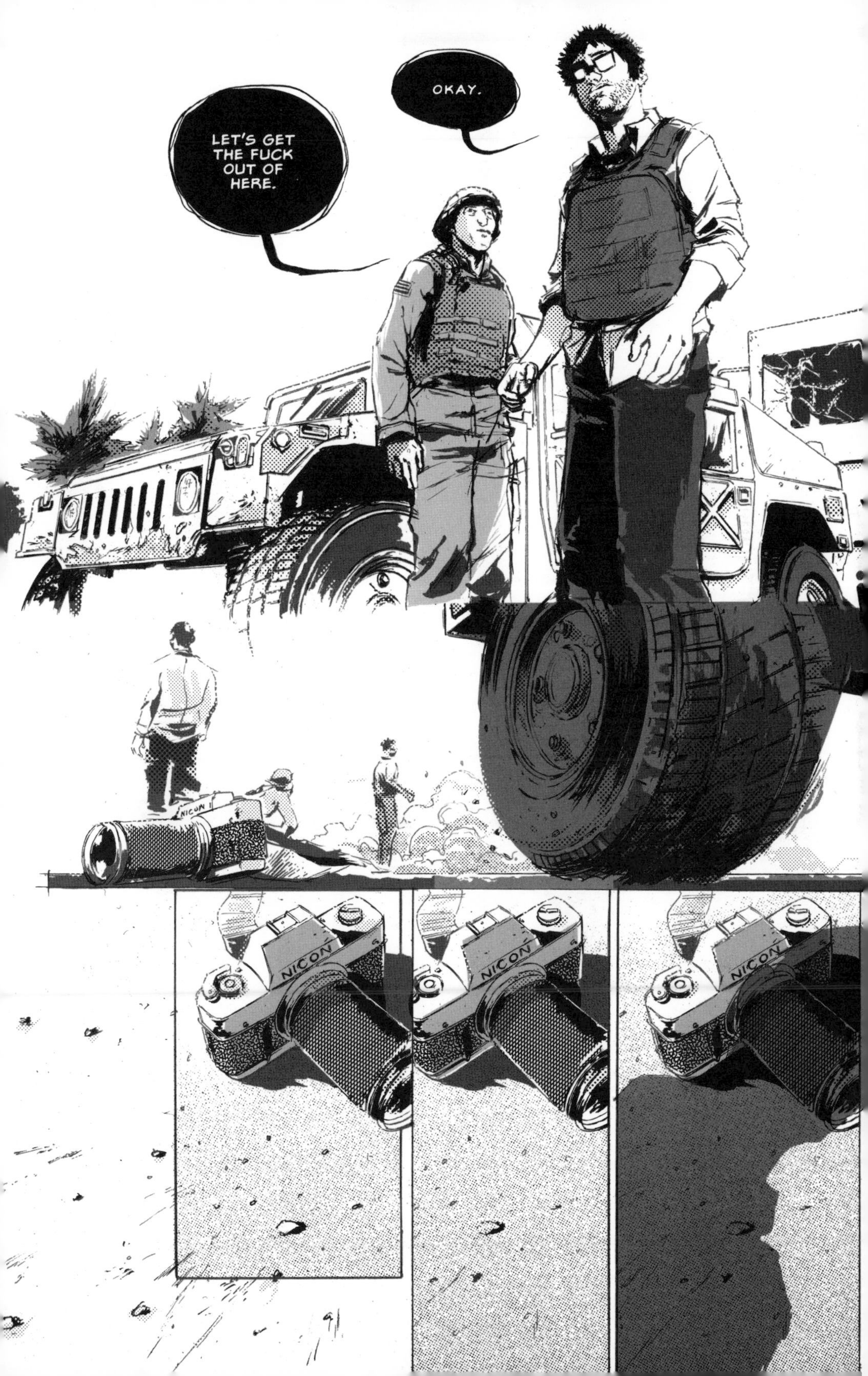
LET'S GET THE FUCK OUT OF HERE.
OKAY.
NICON
NICON
NICON
NICON

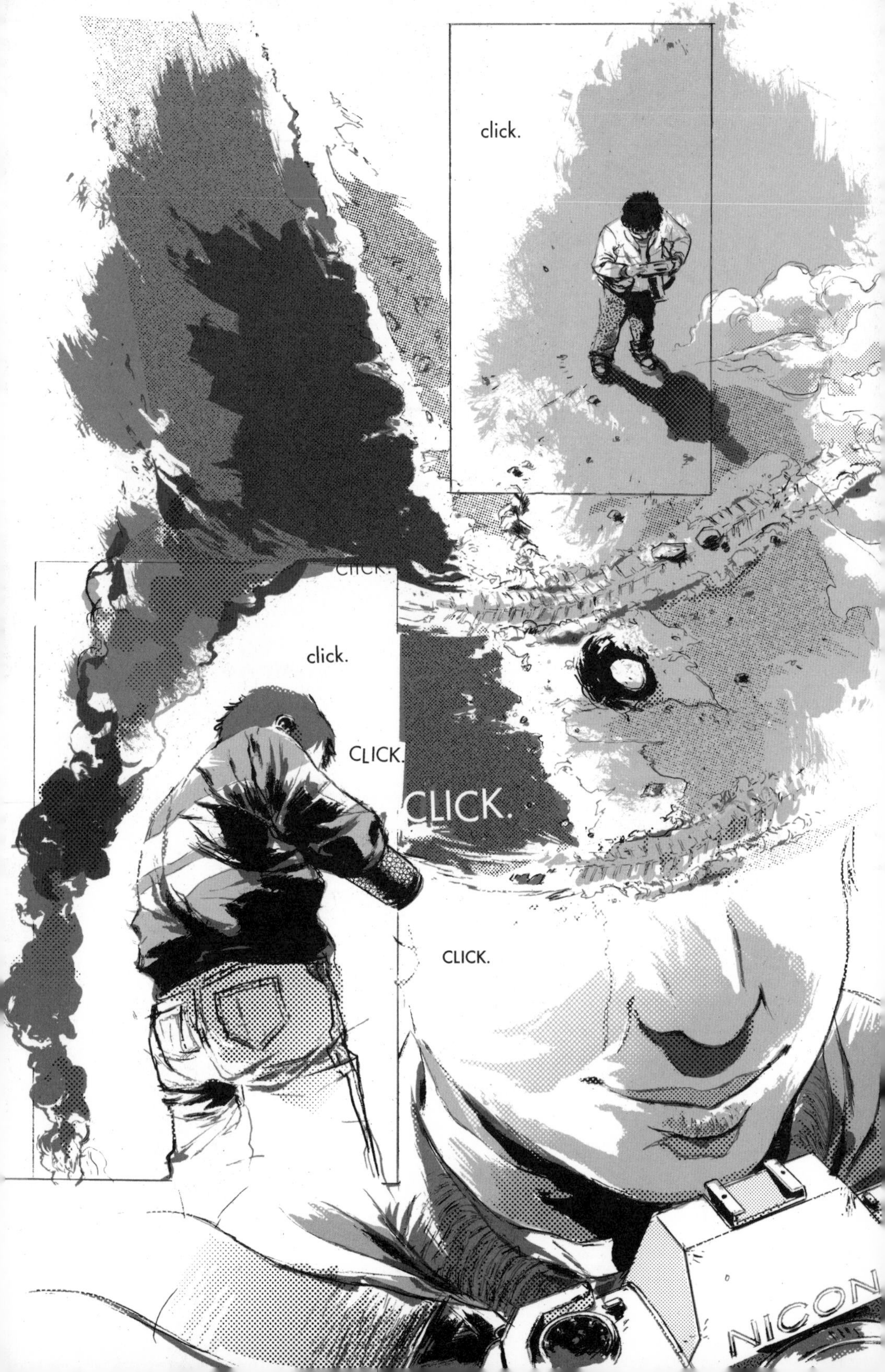
click.
click.
CLICK.
CLICK.
CLICK.
NICON

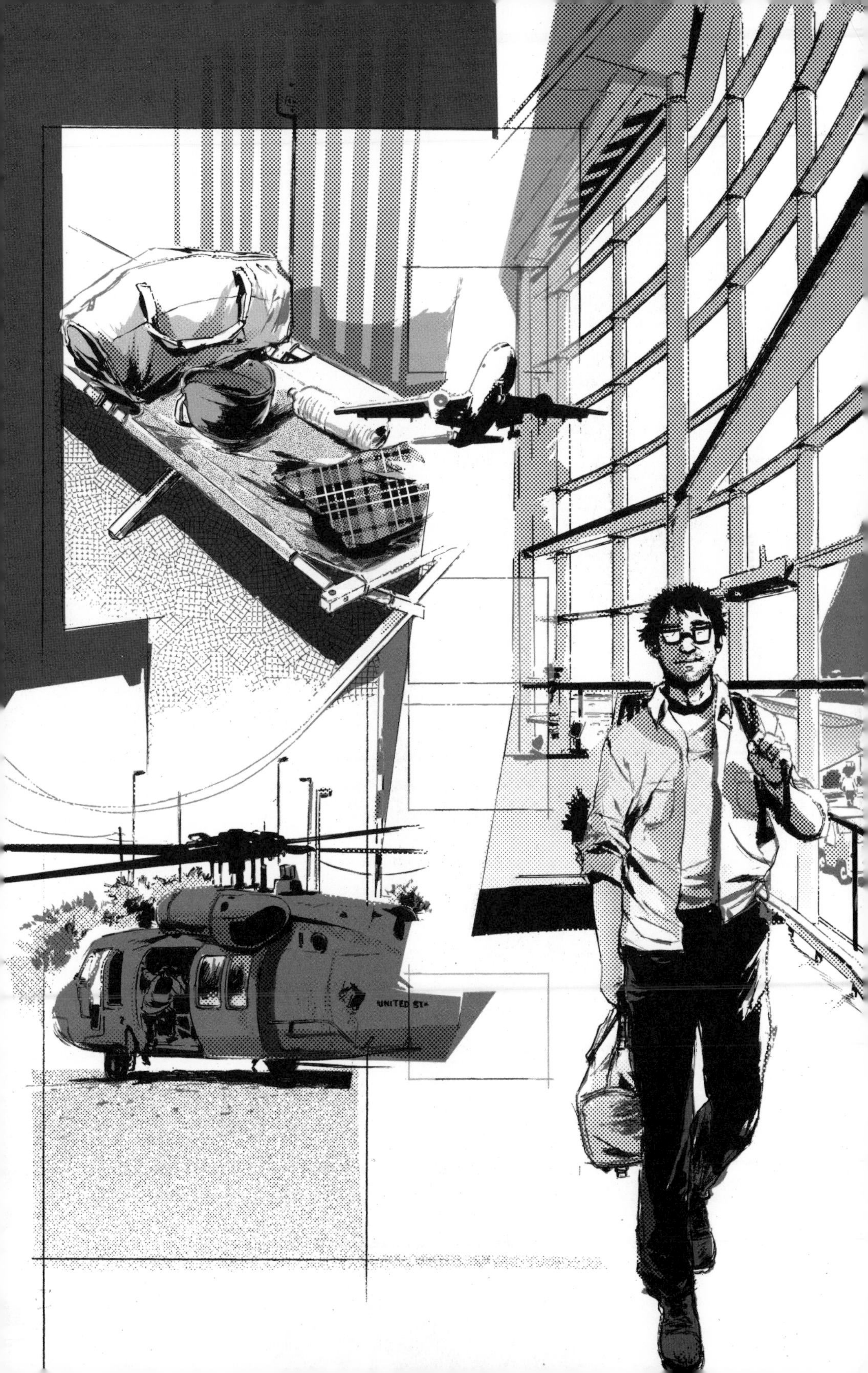
UNITED ST

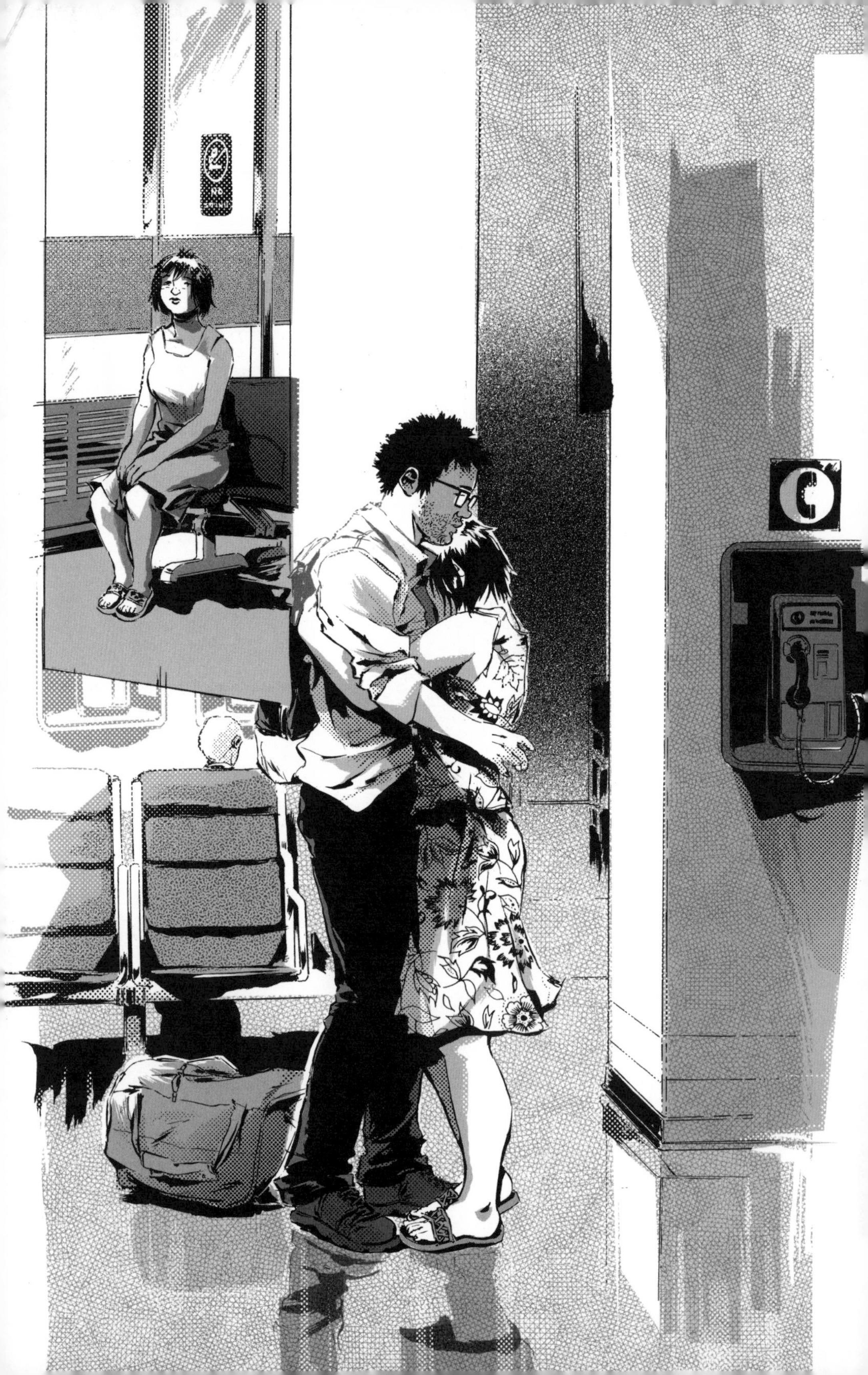
NO

I GOT YOUR LETTERS.
I KNEW I COULD COUNT ON YOU TO UNDERSTAND.
Explosions
shake Iraqi poll places
By DAVID AXE
Staff Writer
YOU'VE BEEN THERE.
YOU KNOW.

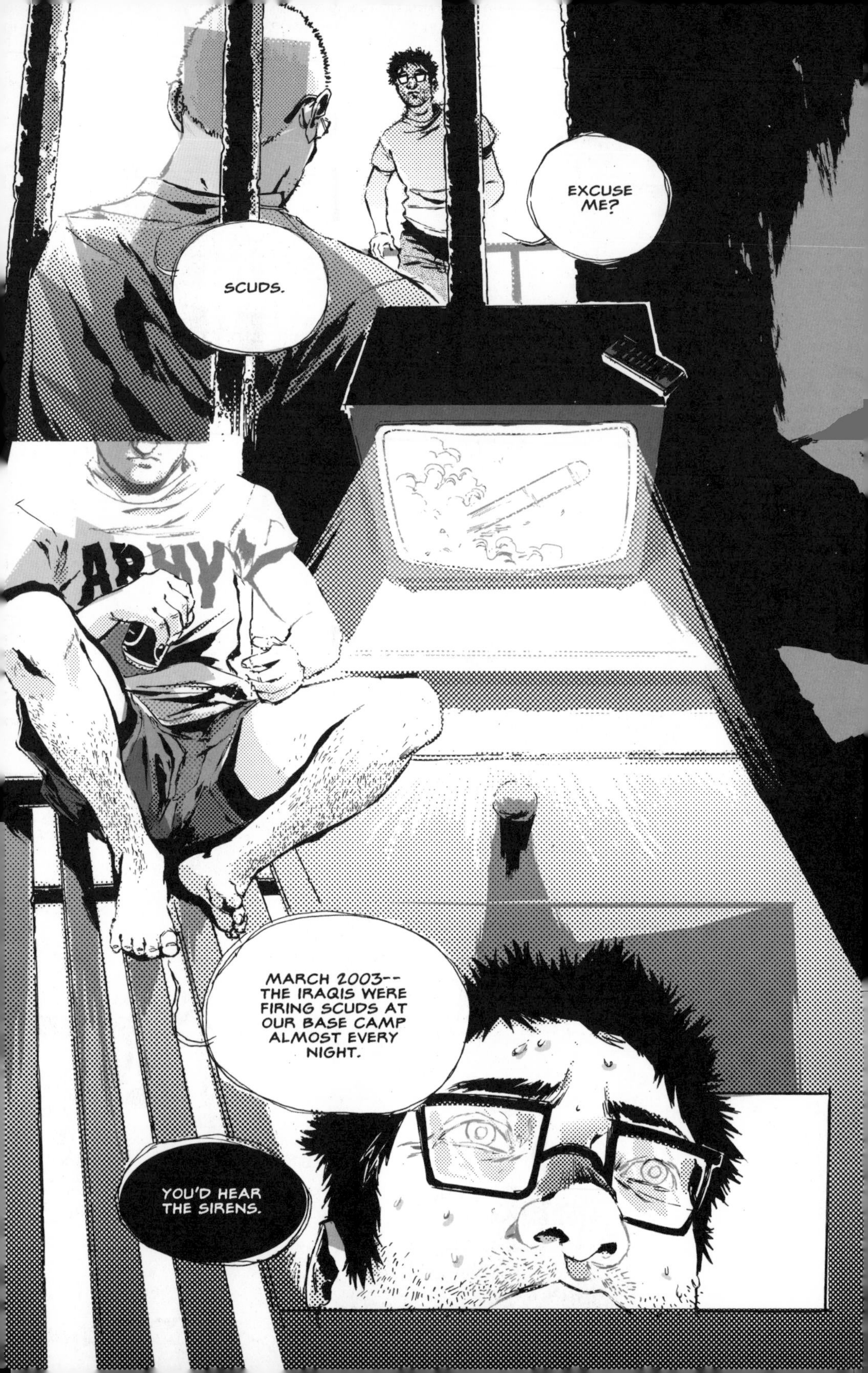
SCUDS.
EXCUSE ME?
ARMY
MARCH 2003--THE IRAQIS WERE FIRING SCUDS AT OUR BASE CAMP ALMOST EVERY NIGHT.
YOU'D HEAR THE SIRENS.

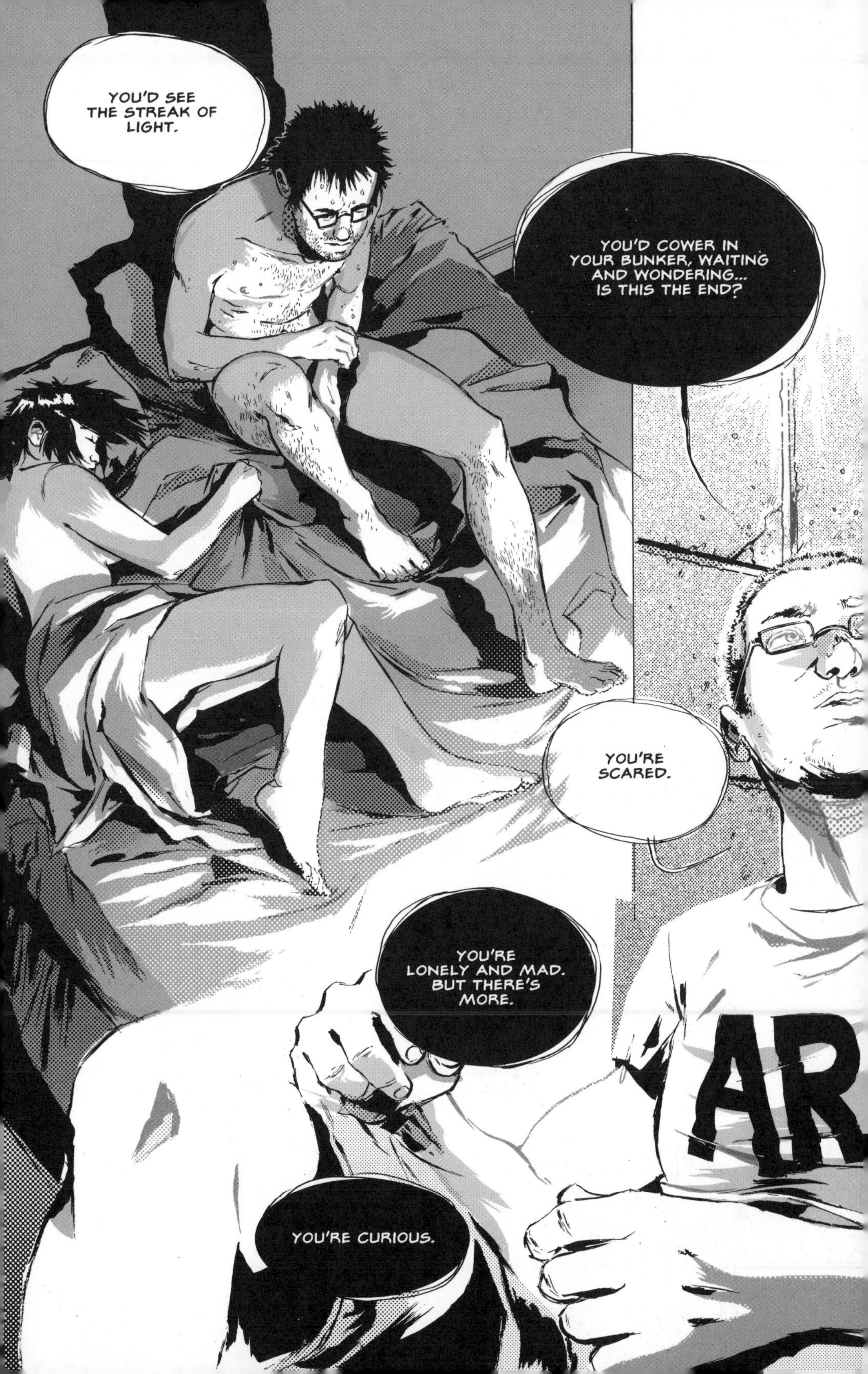
YOU'D SEE THE STREAK OF LIGHT.
YOU'D COWER IN YOUR BUNKER, WAITING AND WONDERING... IS THIS THE END?
YOU'RE SCARED.
YOU'RE LONELY AND MAD. BUT THERE'S MORE.
YOU'RE CURIOUS.
AR

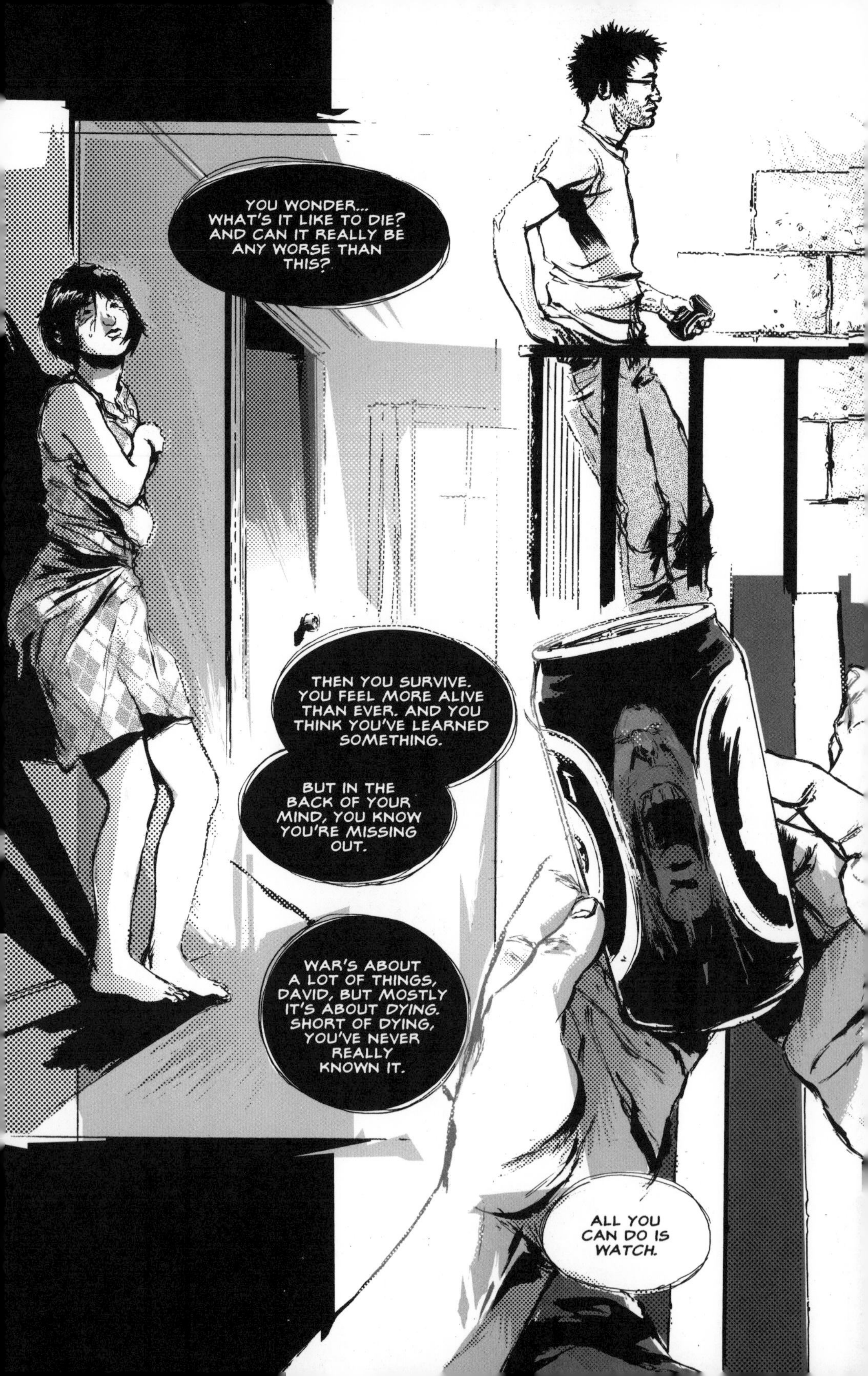
YOU WONDER... WHAT'S IT LIKE TO DIE? AND CAN IT REALLY BE ANY WORSE THAN THIS?
THEN YOU SURVIVE. YOU FEEL MORE ALIVE THAN EVER. AND YOU THINK YOU'VE LEARNED SOMETHING.
BUT IN THE BACK OF YOUR MIND, YOU KNOW YOU'RE MISSING OUT.
WAR'S ABOUT A LOT OF THINGS, DAVID, BUT MOSTLY IT'S ABOUT *DYING*. SHORT OF DYING, YOU'VE NEVER REALLY KNOWN IT.
ALL YOU CAN DO IS *WATCH*.

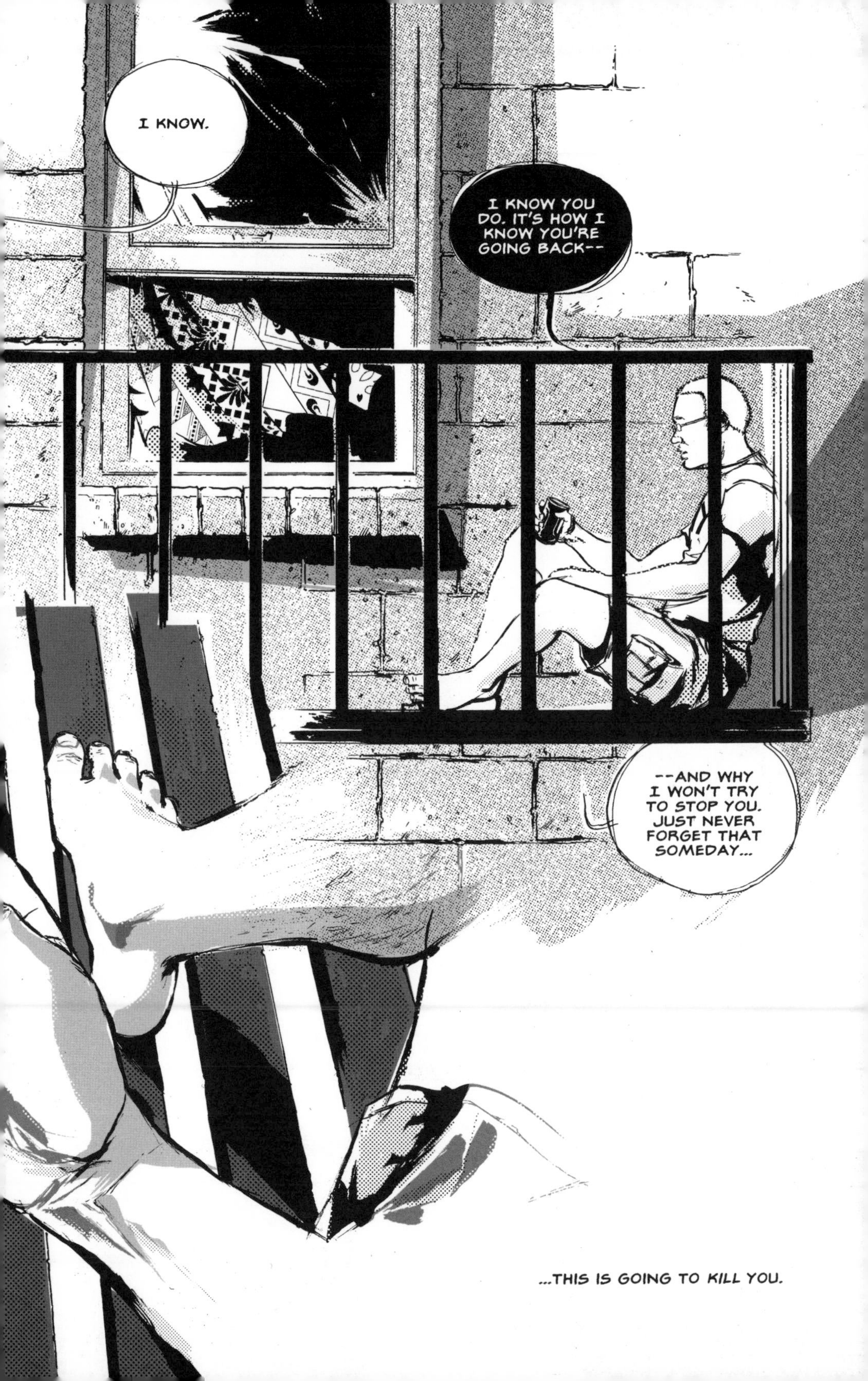
I KNOW.
I KNOW YOU DO. IT'S HOW I KNOW YOU'RE GOING BACK--
--AND WHY I WON'T TRY TO STOP YOU. JUST NEVER FORGET THAT SOMEDAY...
...THIS IS GOING TO KILL YOU.

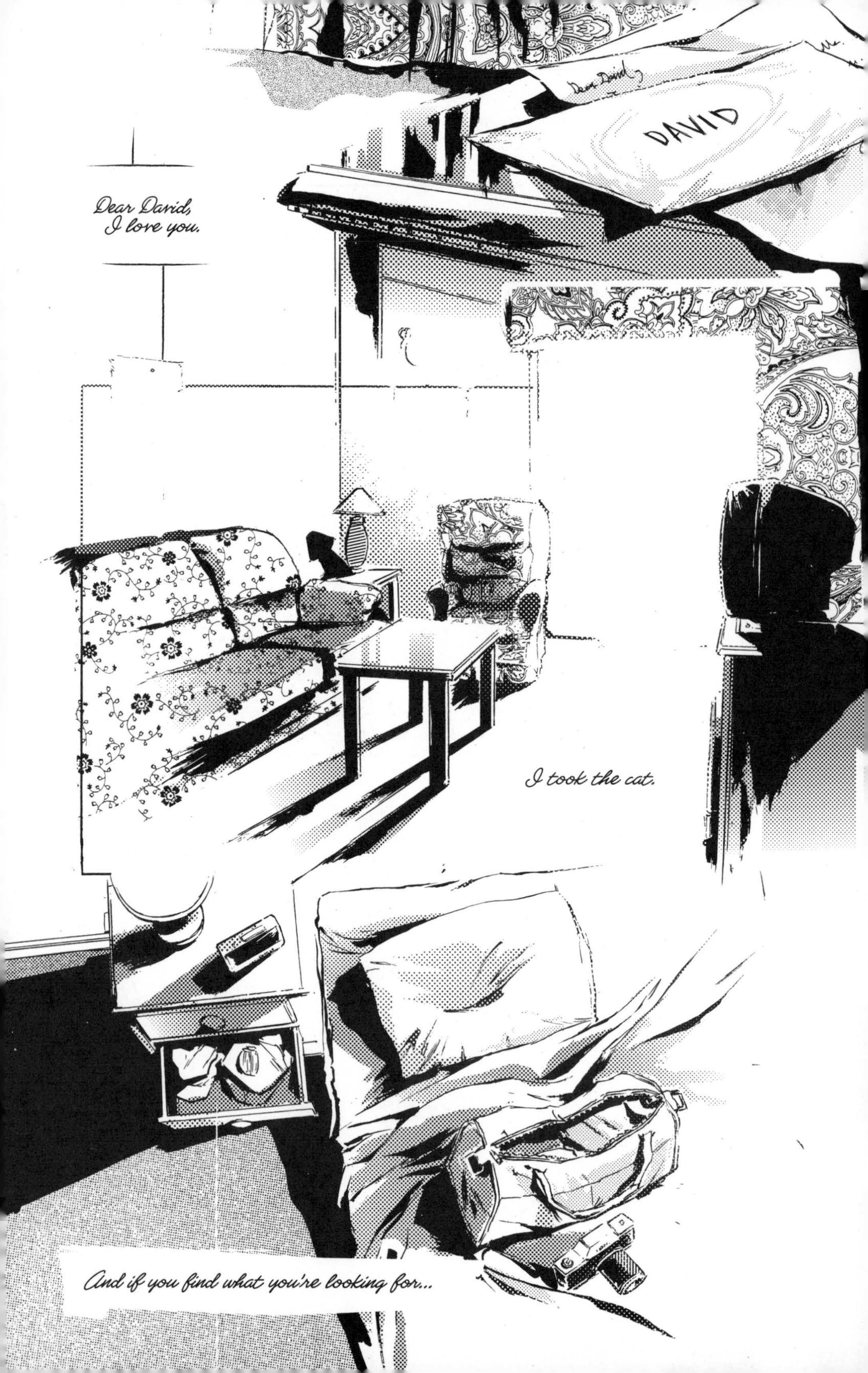
DAVID
Dear David,
I love you.
I took the cat.
And if you find what you're looking for...

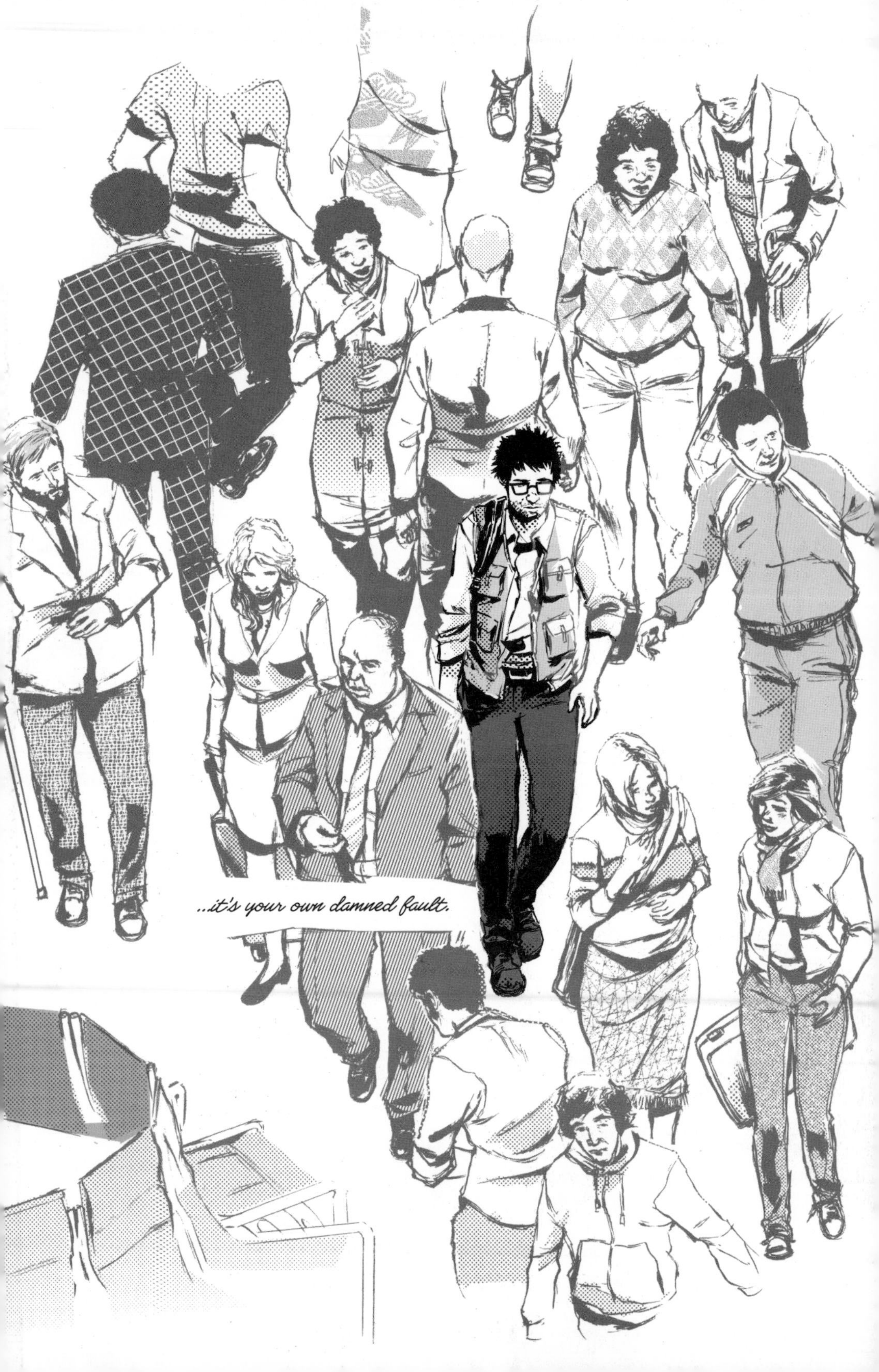
...it's your own damned fault.

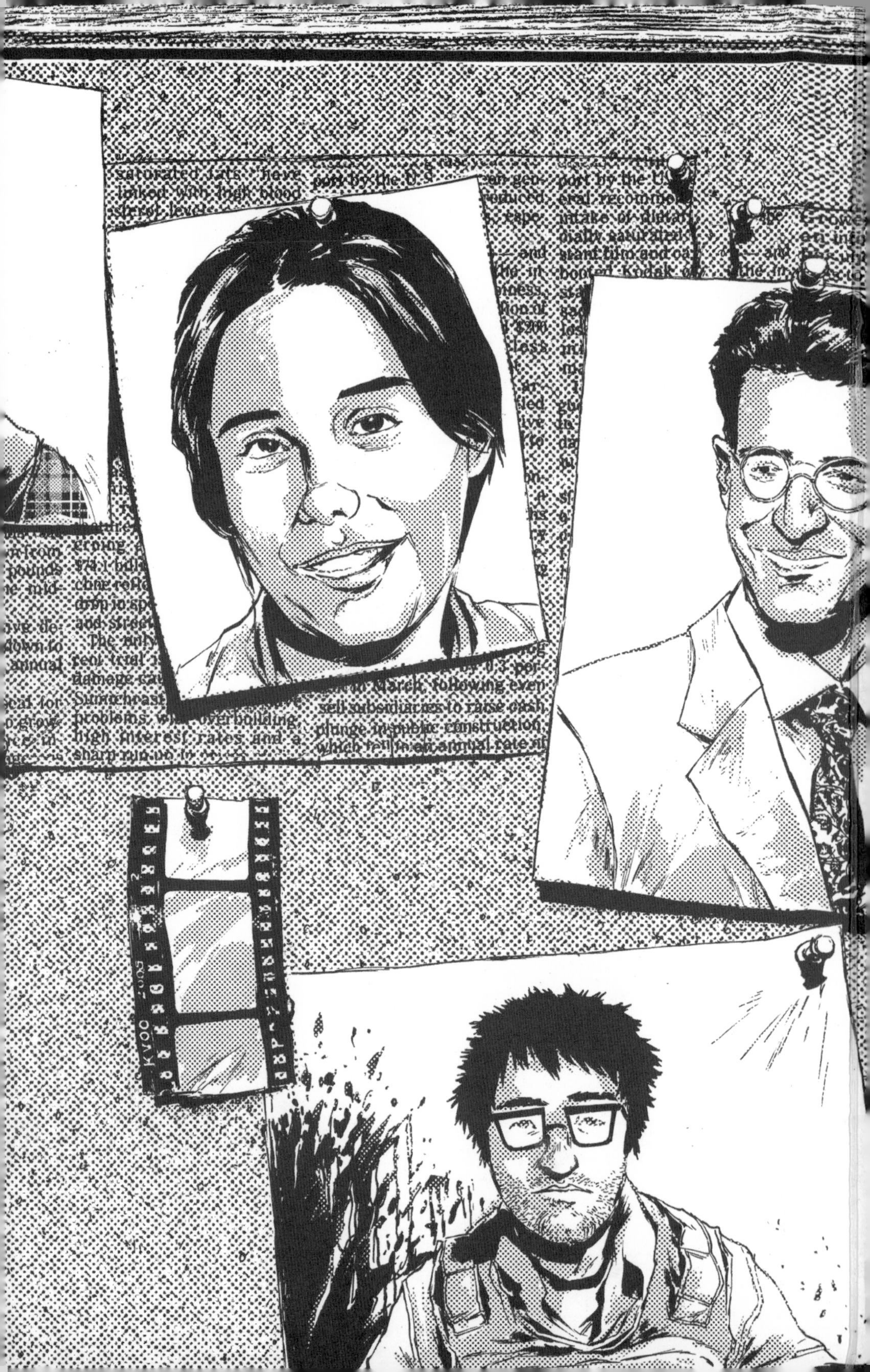

saturated fats have
port by the U.S
problems with overbuilding,
high interest rates and a
sell subsidiaries to raise cash
plunge in public construction,
KVOO